# PRAISE FOR *HOME*

Pastor Tim Diebel and his wife Lori increasingly noticed the unsustainability of our food system. This led to the cognizance that people no longer know how to raise their own food. An interest in food started with date nights spent cooking, voracious reading and learning, and patio gardening at a townhome. The interest became a calling, and Tim resigned after 19 years of service with his church, and he and Lori moved to 10 acres to grow food.

Some glimpses of what he learned:

- Each piece of land has a singular history and makeup.
- Raising food is more complicated than planting, watering, occasional weeding and harvesting.
- Soil requires tender loving care, just like any other living thing.
- Growing food can cause impulsive seed-buying syndrome.
- Gardening is a gateway to trucks, machines, livestock and skills that aren't necessarily innate.
- Tragedies happen in the garden. It is real life, not a glossy catalog.
- Anything at all that grows from our efforts is a gift that should be acknowledged.

This book provides a refreshing perspective that we can all apply to our raising of food as well as how we approach life itself.

*Sally Worley, Executive Director, Practical Farmers of Iowa*

This was certainly an engaging and enjoyable read as it resonates with my experience of significant transitioning to "home." Diebel's descriptions are vivid - initial naiveté, vulnerability, risk-taking, internal and external growth, growing competence and expertise. I liked the inclusion of the informal and formal continuing education he and his wife Lori embraced. Neighbors and willing friends rounded out the community that is growing around them.

Throughout, Tim identifies resources for those who might want beginning places to explore their own transitions. This complements the suggestions toward the end of the book.

Bottom line – *Home by Another Way* is a joy to read.

*Ed Taylor, Sirnoma Farmstead, Illinois*

A s I was reading *Home by Another Way*, I kept being reminded that we need a food system that is part of nature rather than one that tries to control nature.

Diebel's great story and the "spiritual" transformation it describes so well shows that humans and nature are partners who can learn from each other - and that we are not in control. We all need to embrace this important spiritual insight since we are on the cusp of transitioning into the post neo-caloric era. Diebel's great description of how all this is undergirded with "values" and the "relationships" of farmers with nature (p. 27) and ultimately "perennially" designed systems brings the land to light.

I think *Home by Another Way: Harvesting Taproot's Wisdom* is a great contribution to an ecological and spiritual revolution that has begun and over time will continue to thrive, and the future of food and agriculture will be key components of it. This book will increasingly become an important story for any of us interested in food, but especially for the few farmers who are already in the early stages of this spiritual transition and for many more who will make similar transitions in the decades ahead. So, thank you to Tim and Lori Diebel for creating Taproot Garden. And to Tim for making this important contribution to our knowledge and our common transition into a post neo-caloric partnering with nature as we move into the future.

*Fred Kirschenmann, Distinguished Fellow at the Leopold Center,*
*Iowa State University; President of the Board,*
*Stone Barns Center for Food and Agriculture, New York; farmer and philosopher.*

If Tim proves to be as good a farmer and fowler as he is a writer and wordsmith, *Taproot Garden* will blossom and flourish for years. This is a must read for those of us who want to know where our food comes from and who grows it; who long for the day when culture finds its due part in agriculture again; and who are rediscovering the ties between farming and faith, soil and soul.

Tim and Lori have found their day and their way in their place at Taproot Garden.

*Johnny Wray, High Hope Farm, Mississippi*

Humus. Human. Humility. Humor. Each of these words grows out of the Latin word meaning of the soil, the earth. Tim Diebel's book, *Home by Another Way*, is rooted in the earthiness that we feel deeply when digging into the soil with our hands and holding the wetness, the dirtiness, the smell, even the taste that puts us in touch with both the creation and the Creator.

In his book, Tim tells the story of his and Lori's adventure from the worlds of clergy and public school administration into a world of farming. We readers venture with them, sensing our own growing oneness with the soil. A genuine bond grows between writer and reader as we follow Tim and Lori's thoroughly human struggle to thrive in an unfamiliar world. Their innovative tenacity demonstrates an uncommon, but necessary, amount of daily commitment. We find ourselves both challenged and renewed as we see how they learn to bend the knee more deeply in humility before the created order. And, here, too, we see the delight and humor both find embedded in learning how to run a farm and in discovering new ways to relate to the land, to plants, to animals, and to each other.

The Diebels' acreage comes alive for readers as we walk gently with these new farmers who are living out their callings at their small plot of soil called Taproot Garden.

*Roy C. Nilsen, retired Lutheran clergy*

ßß

# HOME BY ANOTHER WAY

## Harvesting Taproot's Wisdom

Blessings,

# Home By Another Way

Harvesting Taproot's Wisdom

Timothy Cap Diebel

Zion Publishing

# Dedication

To my beloved Lori, and what you did – and do – for love.

Seeds are only the beginning of what you sow
and bring to blossom.

I know firsthand of what I speak.

ßß

*Odd as I am sure it will appear to some, I can think of no better form of personal involvement in the cure of the environment than that of gardening. A person who is growing a garden, if he is growing it organically, is improving a piece of the world. He is producing something to eat, which makes him somewhat independent of the grocery business, but he is also enlarging, for himself, the meaning of food and the pleasure of eating.*

Wendell Berry

*What we have heard and known for ourselves must not be withheld from our descendants, but be handed on by us to the next generation.*
Psalm 78:3-4 (Richard Rohr paraphrase)

*Weary or bitter or bewildered as we may be, God is faithful. He lets us wander so we will know what it means to come home.*

Marilynne Robinson

*And having been warned in a dream not to return to Herod, they left for their own country by another road.*

Matthew 2:12 (NRSV)

*Yes, they went home by another way,*
*Home by another way.*
*Maybe me and you can be wise guys, too,*
*And go home by another way.*

Lyrics by James Taylor
From "Home By Another Way"

# CONTENTS

# INTRODUCTION

*I think the whole idea of home is central to who we are as human beings.*

Terry Tempest Williams

Contrary to the assertions of some, home for me has been more portable than fixed. Once upon a time, it was the warmth I knew as a child within my parents' embrace. In later years, it was the shade of a meaningful vocation for which I was comfortably equipped. Home has been the undulating give and take of a loving marriage, and it has been the residential structures within which we have variously parked it.

Those, of course, have been the comfortable times, the centered times. There have been others. Liminal times like Jonah's disconcerting sojourn, in the belly of the fish. Seasons of lostness. Seasons of inquiry when I wandered and wondered and sought fresh answers to old and settled questions. It isn't easy for me to relinquish trusted lenses through which I have viewed and made sense of my foundational, relational, and spiritual surroundings. They frame. They bring a certain clarity. But for all they bring into view, they also obscure.

And so it was, as I describe throughout these pages, that I came to chafe at the constraints of their inadequacy. And that is the word, because it is not so much that those lenses were false, but that they were simply too small, too narrowly focused and therefore misleading, permitting only a certain range of sight. Nudged from within, I set them aside and stepped into the blur of unfamiliarity. It was scary, but it wasn't dangerous. I drifted, but drifted with a net. We had a mortgage, but were otherwise debt-free. We had some savings, and my wife Lori continued in her job that provided income and health benefits for us both. We knew how to ask for help and were no strangers to learning. We have been fortunate to never worry about a roof over our heads or food on our table. Still, it is discomforting and disquieting to leave the familiar environs of the soul, where you have lived and belonged, and follow after a different voice you perceive to be calling your name.

Called, however, I saw no alternative but to answer. And so the adventure began.

# Chapter One

# Change Happens

*Trust the LORD and do good;*
*live in the land, and farm faithfulness.*

Psalm 37:3 (CEB)

W e didn't set out to change our lives. We thought we might help change the world, but it was never our intention to change ourselves. We were simply aspirational and inquisitive professionals who stumbled into a large and provocative curiosity, who became distracted and then intrigued by a glimmer in the night sky of our soul that became a guiding star we could not resist following. The ensuing journey was replete with doubts and dead-ends, with puzzled spirits and sleepless nights wondering where this surprising fixation was leading us. But eventually settling on this simple plot of land that welcomed our questions, our hungers, and our roots changed us, indeed

Lori and I married in the foreground of middle age, well into our respective professions – she, a public school administrator, me, a congregational pastor. Separately, our lives had been busy. Together they were a daily collision. After hours, I had church meetings, while she had supervision duties at athletic events, performances, and parent-teacher conferences. We started our together down time most days at an hour when most households were winding down. We might squeeze in a dinner somewhere between office hours and evening responsibilities, but rarely was a weeknight mutually "free." When one of those magical alignments occurred, the last thing we wanted to do was go out. Besides, going out typically meant running into school parents, who wanted to discuss with Lori a child's progress, or a church member, who wanted to share a concern. Leisure quickly dissolved into work.

Somehow – and neither of us remembers exactly how – we hit upon the idea of cooking as a date night activity. Staying home had the virtue of enabling us to enjoy the home we rarely saw and, more importantly, to relish the high value of private time. Neither of us, however, came into our marriage as cooks. Sure, we prepared meals whenever circumstances required it, but the kitchen was a functional space – a slightly onerous means to a necessary end, employed most often in reheating and reconstituting foods that some factory, somewhere far away, had created and had helpfully enticed us to put it onto our table.

Along the way, however, we became more adventuresome – at least more interested. We tried things. We followed recipes. We purchased better cookware. As our enjoyment deepened and successes outpaced disasters, we began devoting our vacations to honing our kitchen skills: Signing up for "Boot Camps" at the Culinary Institute of America in Hyde Park, New York, and Napa Valley, California; going to immersion schools in Italy, along with classes offered around our own community. Almost before we knew it, we were seriously cooking. And we began to pay attention, not simply to the recipes and the techniques, but to the ingredients themselves that were their raw materials.

We learned that the meats and vegetables, as well as the legumes and grains that find their way into recipes and ultimately onto our tables, are not created equally. Animals are raised in diverse environments, treated according to very different protocols, and nourished using a wide variety of feeds. The produce bins at grocery stores are stocked with vegetables that travel long distances, vegetables selected primarily for their portability and harvested long before their peak maturity. All that we learned before we even thought about the miscellaneous chemicals that had been injected into the flesh, mixed with the feed, or sprayed on the soil and onto the leaves. That was a whole new education.

However our food might have tasted, it ceased to feel very good to us as we cooked it. The food system, as we know it, was becoming to us less and less palatable. It only became more distressing to learn how energy dependent is the whole enterprise. To eat, we have become reliant on inexpensive and plentifully available fuel to manufacture the chemicals, to spread them over the fields; to harvest them, and to transport the goods to market. Given the inevitability that one or both of those enabling factors will eventually go away – availability or affordability – what, I began to wonder, will happen then?

The only answer I could conceive was that we were collectively going to become very, very hungry. A highly undesirable forecast.

A BRIEF, DIGRESSIVE DISCLAIMER IS IN ORDER HERE. None of these observations should be construed as bad-mouthing farmers. Farmers, I have learned, are simply trying to make a living, doing what we have asked them to do, using the tools that the best minds and most credible organizations and governmental authorities have recommended to them. "We have to feed the world," they were told, "and this is how we will do it." Never mind the fact that the evidence now strongly suggests that there are big and unsustainable problems with this philosophy and methodology, farmers rose to the challenge and succeeded (at least in the short term) beyond anyone's wildest imagination. The time has simply come to recognize the longer term implications of those methods and be just as successful teaching and implementing a different way.

Compounding these issues for me was the observation that societally we are becoming increasingly reliant on second-hand nourishment. Yes, I am talking about all those processed foods that jam our market shelves and freezers. But I am also referring to the farm fields that surround us. Where we live in the upper Midwest, enveloped in vast fields of soybeans and field corn, we can claim to be "feeding the world" only in a circuitous sense. We are primarily feeding chickens, hogs, cattle, cars, and processing plants – not people. Yes, our state produces zillions of eggs. And, as any drive through the countryside with the windows down will quickly and odiferously attest, we have more than our share of hog confinements, the output of which we surely do eat. But mostly we are producing ingredients, not food. Factories, largely located elsewhere, are processing and packaging and shipping the bulk of what gets set on dinner tables, along with vegetables grown in massive fields in Florida and California, or flown in from Chile, Argentina, Mexico, and beyond.

At least until we can no longer afford all that processing and distribution.

Someone had better remember how to grow food on different terms, I thought to myself.

Though I didn't comprehend it at the time, in that observation a seed was sown that eventually would blossom into the conviction that I must locate myself within that life-sustaining circle of memory.

There was only one problem: I had nothing to remember. Having lived in cities my entire life, I had never grown anything except a record collection. I had never planted a garden, and (if I am completely honest) I thought of myself as above all that. Food came from supermarkets and drive-through windows. I knew nothing about soil. I had spent my life in classrooms earning degrees and in offices earning a salary. I knew nothing of planting a seed and nurturing it toward a harvest. I was good at preaching sermons and tying bowties and officiating at weddings and funerals, but I knew nothing about wielding a hoe or recognizing plant or poultry diseases or differentiating between good insects and bad or discouraging rabbits and moles and deer. The very idea of entering into such an undertaking was as laughable as it was ludicrous.

But, before I knew what was happening, my reading list began to change – from Tillich's *Systematic Theology* to Gene Logsdon's *Holy Shit: Managing Manure to Save Mankind* – and the nuances and strategies for sustainable food production dominated my days and unsettled my nights. I began to feel guilty about accepting a salary under false pretenses, and, increasingly, I felt called to this other kind of pursuit – a ministry of its own. I more and more came to realize, it was one of very different shape and substance.

So, it was that, with Lori's blessing, I convened a meeting with the congregation's officers and announced my resignation. After all the years we had shared together, they knew me well enough that they couldn't help but snicker at the absurdity of my new direction. But they were supportive, understanding, and indulgent, and sent us off with a fond farewell and the gift of a wheel-barrow and a pair of overalls.

In the intervening months, a realtor friend had helped us locate an acreage a few miles out of town with a nice house and ten acres of land to live out this calling. Feeling a little like the family in the old television sitcom *The Beverly Hillbillies* in reverse, we loaded up the truck and moved to the country.

GOD HELP US ALL.

# CHAPTER TWO

# THE OUTWARD MOVE

*Well he's one of those who knows that life*
*Is just a leap of faith*
*Spread your arms and hold your breath*
*And always trust your cape*

Guy Clark

I certainly knew that I was jumping off of everything that felt familiar and secure – education, years of experience, a job, an income – but, though I wasn't aware of any cape tied around my neck that would help me fly, I was strangely, perhaps irrationally, confident. So it was that I jumped. Never mind that I was too young to collect a pension or cash in an IRA even if I had had one. Which is to say that "we" jumped together, because, in every possible sense of the word, I couldn't do it alone. We left a comfortable townhouse in the heart of the city, where cultural amenities were minutes away and someone else mowed grass and cleared snow, and moved to a farmstead five miles out of town, on a road the last mile and a half of which wasn't paved.

Looking back, it seems like it all happened overnight. The more granular truth is that my ultimate resignation from the position I had held for the prior 19 years and our move to the country represent the giant leap, culminating a series of baby steps we didn't even know we were taking.

There was, for example, a failed vacation that turned seminal.

We had scheduled time away from work, arranged coverage for our respective responsibilities, and solidified our plans. There was a professional conference to attend in a neighboring state, putting us within tourist reach of some sightseeing that had interested us. I sent in our registrations for the conference, developed a driving route, made hotel reservations for the duration of the lengthy excursion, and then gave our anticipation full permission to build. Weary and stressed, both of us needed a vacation, and this one felt long overdue.

Then we received some disturbing news. Lori's dad, who had been experiencing some health challenges, was going to need an aortic valve replacement – a procedure now scheduled squarely in the midst of our carefully planned vacation. Suddenly the longed-for leisure didn't seem quite so important. We canceled our conference registrations, canceled our various hotel reservations, and prepared to camp out around a Minnesota hospital instead.

And then, another twist. At the last minute a minor but intervening infection forced a several-week delay in the planned surgery. So there we were with two weeks of blocked out vacation time, a trashcan full of canceled plans and arrangements, and nothing to do on such short notice. At least nothing that our frazzled minds and spent energies could conceive and develop on such short notice. The one thing we were sure of was that we were not aborting our time away from work.

And then an idea began to emerge.

Our townhouse was functionally a one level home, but it had a finished and furnished basement level that was essentially a suite unto itself. It featured a large living area with comfortable lounge seating and TV, a cozy bedroom, and full bath plus the laundry facilities. All it lacked was a kitchen. What if we closed the blinds on the main level, and lived downstairs in relative anonymity? We could pretend we were anywhere, catch up on the leisure reading we had been neglecting for too long to remember, sneak upstairs to prepare meals, and remain undisturbed, because everyone would think we were away. It was, perhaps, a naive conception; but being the only idea we had, we acquiesced with a shrugging, "Why not?"

The simple "staycation" that unfolded became one of those little but transformative baby steps, though I suspect few were fooled by our faux absence. We read – all kinds of things, but chiefly among them Barbara Kingsolver's *Animal, Vegetable, Miracle,* which had been published a couple of years before. Initially I was reading the book, but I interrupted Lori's own reading so often with excerpts I wanted her to hear that she eventually abandoned her own selections to join me in Kingsolver's immersion into growing food and eating locally. In the appendix was a compendium of resources designed to enable the reader to continue the exploration. Our mental and culinary appetites whetted, we explored – first online and then locally. We discovered the concept of CSA's (Community Supported Agriculture programs that sell shares in the harvest of their vegetable farms). Most, by this time in the year, were fully booked up, but two welcomed us. We visited. We talked. We got acquainted. We got dirt on our shoes. By vacation's end we had written membership checks to both, and over the subsequent months remaining in the season, we were overwhelmed with weekly boxes of greens and squashes and peppers and tomatoes, herbs and cucumbers and curiosities neither of us recognized.

But we ate. We ate very well. And we fell in love with the abundance and the fresh experience of a nourishment that went beyond our stomachs and extended to our very souls. Slowly we began to look at food less as mere "ingredient" and more as precious gift, as the very evocation of soil and substance and creation and the vibrancy of life itself. But even this ground-shifting experience apparently had antecedents.

I no longer recall what I had been reading or what stick had been stirring my thinking, but looking back over the weeks preceding this seminal space, it's clear that seeds had somehow found fertile soil. My sermon from the Sunday just prior to the start of our vacation was titled, "Sowing Holy Seeds," and included phrases like:

> *"God is doing a new thing – casting shade from unexpected trees – and we are invited, as people of faith, to find ourselves beneath their branches," and "I look around us at all the holy seeds that we are holding in our hands and have already strewn around and grow silent with the wonder. Who knows what shoots and stems might be emerging around us even now? And who can anticipate the taste of the fruit?" The morning prayer that day confessed that, "while we work to get life buttoned down, you, God, sprout a sprig in the midst of the pavement and furnish new shade where we would least expect it."*

Neither one of us had any idea what sprig was about to sprout in our pavement. But when it began to emerge we surprised ourselves by watering it, sheltering it, and encouraging it to grow. We ate, we learned, we read still more and dreamed of the possibilities. At least I did. Lori is much more sensible than I am – practical and down to earth. Yes, we were changed by that simple but extravagant staycation, but we had jobs to do, expectations to satisfy, bills to pay, careers to advance, and retirements to fund. And so we returned to work – at least part of me did. Part of me remained to the side, indulging this new perspective and how it had come to claim us.

The second baby step would have to wait another year. A friend of ours serves a church in Kansas City, which has an all-congregation reading program they call "Building Community Book by Book." That year they had been reading together one of the novels by Wendell Berry who, through his essays, poetry and fiction, has become one of the most outspoken and influential patriarchs of the sustainable agriculture movement. With the encouragement of a like-minded clergy friend, I had begun reading his discomforting but strangely resonant books and was excited to learn that the church was not only reading him, they were planning an evening with him to talk directly about the novel, but also about his work more broadly. There would be a presentation, then a time for Q&A, and then an interactive reception. Knowing we might be interested, my friend invited us to join in the evening.

A three-hour drive after work on a Thursday evening is not our usual routine, but the conversation in the car crackled with anticipation as we hurried south on the freeway. I had stowed a worn copy of one of Berry's books in the unlikely case I could snag an autograph. I self-consciously carried it inside as we found our place among the pews.

It was a magical evening. We had scored an invitation to Mount Olympus – a view to which Berry would surely roll his eyes and suggest that we "get a grip" – but, I was more than a little starstruck and deeply moved. As we pointed the car back north again, autographed book tucked in Lori's purse, we somehow knew that the earth had shifted beneath us yet again. Along the miles and through the hours of that drive home we spoke aloud the hypothetical image of the Diebels on a farm. Maybe not actually a "farm," but on some amenable plot of ground where we, in partnership with the land, could explore and apply something of what we were learning; could embrace and indeed embody something of who we were becoming. It was an idea – perhaps even a barely conceivable vision – but, on that trip, we spoke it aloud.

And as the biblical book of Genesis suggests, when words are spoken out loud, new worlds are created.

Life, however, with its manifold and incumbent obligations, has a way of wrestling attentions back down to earth. We had jobs that demanded our energies and more immediate focus. We went back to work – Lori, addressing school district issues; I, preaching sermons, setting out programming, and offering pastoral care. But if we were quickly back under the water of daily details, our imaginations managed to poke a straw up through the surface and breathe in sustaining air.

I have no idea how we learned of Practical Farmers of Iowa, apart from that mystical way the universe seems to send out sparks of connection at just the right moments for those in whom it has sensed some readiness. "PFI," as it is more familiarly known, is a non-profit organization dedicated to the support and education of farmers in the region with a bent toward sustainability. An agricultural "big tent," PFI works with both organic and conventional farmers, fruit and vegetable growers right alongside commodity crop and livestock farmers, inviting a shared concern for the land and what it produces and sustains. And for each other. A whole calendar of "field days" scheduled throughout the year invites members to various farms to learn about some exemplary practice or research project or system or tool, along with webinars, social events, interest groups, and an annual conference.

The annual conference, held at a centrally located convention facility, features keynote speakers, dozens of workshops, discussion groups, and social times over a two-day period in the dead of winter.

A few months after our magical evening with Wendell Berry, our radar lit up with news of the upcoming Practical Farmers of Iowa annual event, scheduled for that January in Marshalltown, a couple of hours away. We downloaded the brochure, scrutinized the program plans, and noticed a couple focused on "beginning farmers."

"Hmm," we responded.

And then went back to work.

Like gum on the bottom of our shoe, however, I couldn't seem to shake the preposterous idea of attending the conference. We returned to the brochure. We looked back over the workshop options. And, before our more sensible natures could block the step, we sent in our registrations, reserved hotel space, and requested another vacation day from our employers.

Among the offerings on the first day of the conference was a "beginning farmer luncheon," but guessing that such a social affair was intended for those beginners who already *were* farming, we timidly concluded that we didn't qualify. We did circle the entry for the "beginning farmer workshop" later that afternoon – a three-hour block that, according to the printed description, would offer information, mentoring, guided planning, and more. After satisfying our own lunch needs and checking into the hotel, we made our way to the conference site, picked up our folders and name tags, and hunted down the room that would be our focus for the afternoon, where a couple dozen other self-assessed beginning farmers gathered alongside of us.

Preliminaries ensued – speaker introductions, an overview of the time we would spend, et cetera – after which we were invited to pair up with someone we didn't know, spend a few minutes getting acquainted, and then introduce our partner to the rest of the group. I've long since forgotten the generous young man who introduced me by noting that I farmed "less than an acre," but his generosity was quickly tarnished by Lori's partner who introduced her with the humorous clarification that she… "is married to Tim, and that 'less than an acre' they farm is the deck of their urban townhouse.'"

Busted in the first 15 minutes of the workshop.

Nonetheless, it was an informative afternoon. Along the way sheets of butcher paper and colored markers were distributed and we were invited to sketch out the farming operation we imagined. We had no idea. We hadn't actually thought about anything so practical.

But that was likely the point of the exercise: to begin to visualize some kind of potential reality, around which to coalesce some evaluation, assessment, planning and consideration. We sketched in a large garden – that would be a priority – and a tool shed. We imagined a hoop house (one of those structures made of hoops stuck into the ground at regular intervals with plastic stretched over the top) and maybe a pond and some fruit trees of multiple varieties. Oh, and a house with big wisdom.

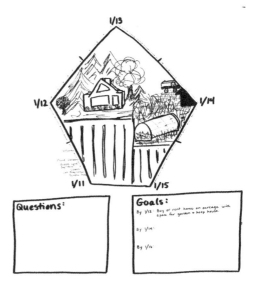

We would live on this mythical property, rooting in ourselves as well as our vegetables. Would there be livestock? We didn't think so. Would there be woods? We hoped so. Eventually we divided into small groups, each one mentored by experienced farmers, and shared our sketchy plans. More than once questions were raised about "sales" and "profitability" and "scale." We blithely responded that those weren't relevant issues Our plan was simply to learn.

We were uniformly met with blank and incredulous stares, as if to say, "Oh, you poor, poor misguided fools."

Armed with our butcher paper sketch and our weekend's worth of workshop notes, we returned to the city and inserted ourselves again into the swirl of our lives. Quickly the conference "buzz" was drowned out by more imminent necessities and pragmatisms as we settled back into our townhouse with its "less than an acre" deck farm.

The townhouse community in which we lived had a few vacant lots collectively owned primarily to prevent commercial development out our windows. In our after-conference enthusiasm we wondered, first to ourselves and subsequently to the association board, whether that vacant space might be used for garden plots. We had heard of community gardens around town – including at a retirement complex for seniors that I routinely visited – and wondered if others of our neighbors might value the space to sow a few seeds. We knew several of our neighbors nursed pots of tomatoes and peppers and heirloom beans on their tiny decks, as did we.

"No," was the quick answer. For various reasons the idea was dismissed out of hand. It seemed silly to me. It was, after all, simply grass-covered land in ample acreage to accommodate any number of possibilities. But our idea went the way of so many ideas, both good and bad: dying for lack of a "second."

But we must have talked out loud about our recent experiences and emerging dreams, within hearing range of our friends. Most of them politely indulged our fantasy or laughed. There were, however, others who listened beyond the absurdity. A couple of weeks beyond the conference, about the time we were rolling up our butcher paper fantasy "map" to forget about in a closet, an email hit our "inbox" from some friends who live on a family farm almost an hour northeast of town.

*From: "Shirley Hanson & Larry Ladd"*

*To: "Tim Diebel"*

*Sent: Sunday, January 30, 2011 10:03:15 AM GMT -06:00 US/ Canada Central*

*Subject: Land for Farming*

*Without going into a long winded E-mail.*

*We would like to support your effort in farming.*

*Why not do it out here and give it a one year trial?*

*We'll pick some land around the out buildings, till up the grass with my tractor, etc.*

*You will have water, a place to store tools, a place for a burn pile, and us (LOL).*

*Your thoughts? Larry*

Stunned at the generosity, we shed a tear or two and after fifteen minutes of "Wow" and "Do you think…" and "Maybe we could…," we accepted their offer. Then, turning on our computers, we began browsing online seed catalogues and dreaming. This vision was beginning to take shape.

As spring approached, I did, indeed, visit our benefactors' farm, where we walked around the near-environs and evaluated possible spaces. One was too far away from water, while another suffered from too much shade. Finally, the just-right "Goldilocks" plot emerged with only one liability that I could anticipate. It was essentially the primary green space outside the back door of the house, in looming view of the residents who enjoy beauty and meticulous upkeep. I drove away with equal parts elation, anticipation, and a heavy sense of responsibility for maintaining the aesthetics of the property. Meticulous weeding would have to be a top priority and, therefore, an unending task.

We understood, however, that this was a temporary fix. Assuming a successful trial, we would eventually want a garden of our own, which by now we recognized would necessitate a move.

Of some sort.

On this point, we discovered, we agreed in principle but differed on details. I envisioned an acreage in the country. Lori saw a conventional home in some congenial neighborhood with an adequate yard in which I could play. We talked. We listened. We weighed pros and cons. We heard what we wanted to hear. We probed the wisdom of our friends, most of whom thought we were crazy and counseled Lori to just "say no to the madness." We deferred decisions to another day.

At least we deferred locational decisions. Others were thundering louder and louder in our heads, like the question of my continuing employment. Several factors were coalescing that nudged us toward clarity. I had served in this current position for 19 years. During those years the church and I had climbed steep mountains together, gasped for breath, struggled under water, soared, celebrated, and gained strength. We had shared precious experiences, created together exhilarating expressions of what we understood ministry to be, reimagined, remodeled, branched out, and made big strides. It had been, in every professional way, enlarging and enlivening and good. But by this time, I was feeling spent – weary with what it was, and wearier still with what it necessarily would yet be. It was time in this congregation's life for yet another new beginning and I was clearer and clearer that I had neither the interest nor the energy for it.

Meanwhile, I was feeling increasingly called to this new application. "Call," in my line of work, has always been a large and powerful concept. Clergy bristle at the idea of being "hired." We are "called." This sense of an inner, but immanently holy, nudging voice is at the core of the word "vocation." While not limited to the religiously inclined, religious communities tend to be the theaters in which this vocational language is most volubly spoken. We don't simply seize opportunities as a matter of whim or wish, according to this belief system, nor do we act on our own initiative, but rather we respond to a nudging and compelling voice. We answer a call. Just as I could truthfully acknowledge that every prior professional move had resulted from a clear discernment of such a nudge, so can I attest that this fresh and seemingly bizarre turning was in response to a call that sounded equally compelling, and one to which I was increasingly powerless to say "no."

Did I hear actual voices? No. Could anybody else verify it? Hardly. But then, that has never been the case. Read through the stories of vocational prodding in scripture and you'll find that it's always a pretty lonely proposition. Is it heartburn, or a holy voice? No one is finally able to help sort that out apart from the one most torn by the need for discernment. Ultimately, however, the sense of it is as inexplicable and indefensible as it is undeniable.

There, I found myself called in a fresh direction. Lori, open if not eager, trusting if not quite enthusiastic, encouraging but questioning, lovingly acquiesced. In the days following the church's Easter celebrations, I convened our leaders and announced my resignation. Saying the words, I thought I was going to suffocate, faint, or cry. Thankfully, it only turned out to be two of the three.

It wouldn't happen for a while. I had closure to bring at work. We had plans to make for our old home – and for a new home. We had no tangible means, after all, to implement this new and laughable vocational application save that famous "less-than-an-acre" deck garden and a borrowed plot of ground an hour away. We had landed ourselves in a strange and disorienting state of animated suspension, somehow confident – Naively? Delusionally? – that it would all work out.

Over the subsequent weeks we tilled new ground – agriculturally, professionally, relationally, maritally – and tried our best to live into whatever it was that was unfolding, even if we only benefited from the thinnest clue as to what it might be.

We visited a few acreages – one, a historic home that had been on the Underground Railroad; another with an old farmhouse with water in the basement. Nothing really called our name. We learned from our friends who were sponsoring our trial garden that a property nearby had recently come on the market. We were curious. We were open. We called the number for the listing realtor posted on the sign and made arrangements to visit. Looking back, the house and property occasioned a preposterous exploration. Everything about it was too big; but, then, everything about this new venture seemed too big to comprehend. We turned off the county road onto the property's driveway and followed the long and winding lane through trees and around a 3-acre lake, scenically accessorized by a small cabin whose picturesque front porch extended out over the water to a tie-up for a rowboat. We drove on through an open meadow to the house, which was adjacent to the horse barn and chicken coop, beside the swimming pool, surrounded by lilac trees.

We followed the realtor inside, through the canning kitchen, into the large main kitchen where we began the tour. I'll not belabor the details, save reporting that the house featured four bedrooms, a movie theater, and an office. There were 30-acres in all, a mix of woodlands, meadow and lake. I was instantly smitten and bedazzled. Somehow, if I cocked my head just right, it reminded me of Tuscany. Lori didn't say much.

In the following weeks we returned to the property two additional times, once in the company of a dear friend, who had operated the bed and breakfast in whose backyard garden we had been married, to assess the viability of the house for use as a bed and breakfast. Mentally, I had already moved in. Lori, unsure, agreed to submit an offer. We contacted our own realtor to manage the details on our behalf, and waited. And prayed. I learned later that, while I prayed for the offer to be accepted, Lori was fervently lobbying the Divine toward the opposite outcome.

She, and as it turned out, God, recognized the absurdity of the idea. The property was vastly more than we had any business trying to manage. The house, while magnificent, was far too big and poorly located for a bed and breakfast – as if we had any business operating a business anyway. We had no real interest in owning a swimming pool. And it was all a long distance removed from Lori's work – you know, the work that would be our only source of income. The long, meandering driveway would be a monster to maintain in winter, and the drive into town would be tedious in the best of weather; perilous in the worst.

In truth, we only had to wait about 15 minutes for a response. Our purchase offer, though at the top of our financial capacity, was a low-ball offer compared to the asking price. It was rejected out of hand, and we had no recourse for a counter. I was grieved; Lori, relieved. We settled back into our transition.

Our realtor, however, had other ideas. He respected a courteous "grieving period" after the real estate rejection before letting us know that he had some other properties for us to consider. By this time, he understood the kind of property we hoped to find—and understood our financial capacity. He scheduled appointments, we visited first one property some distance west of town, and then another. These we easily dismissed for miscellaneous reasons, and then we drove up the driveway of a property south of town. Situated on ten acres, the farmstead featured a lovely house built a little over a decade before by the current owners, a large metal building with a bathroom and a heater, a garden shed, several acres of open prairie and woodlands. Inside, the house featured warm wood, wide windows, open spaces, a large and updated kitchen and an intangibly good feeling. We liked it, sure, but our heads were numbing by this time and we retreated. Too soon after our earlier rejection, we feared falling in love "on the rebound."

Thank you, but no, thank you.

A week went by. The house and the property smoldered in our sub-conscious, occasionally flaming up into the foreground of our respective imaginations and shared conversations. We danced around it. We looked the other way. We busied ourselves with other things. We drove out of town for an overnight holiday indulgence where, in the quiet seclusion of a restored suite in a historic hotel, we allowed the subject its honest moment.

And then we called the realtor and scheduled another visit.

This time around we asked different questions. We looked with more honest eyes and allowed more critical assessments. We picked apart, we reassembled, we closed our eyes and imagined, we took stock of how our souls were experiencing the space.

And we liked how it felt.

We smiled.

We took a deep breath.

And we made an offer.

There was some back-and-forth negotiation, but ultimately a deal was struck. We would become the newest stewards of a property whose title reached back to 1848, a few years after a treaty was signed with the tribe who had been its longer-term residents. What its new chapter would look like was yet to take shape. All we knew was that it would include the two of us.

In the meantime, we had work to do. We had a townhouse to sort and organize into boxes, and ultimately to sell.

ßß

CHAPTER THREE

# PUTTING DOWN ROOTS

*Go from your country and your kindred and your father's house to the land that I will show you.*

Genesis 12:1 (NRSV)

W hat an interesting concept – property. Places have discernible character and location, but less clear is our own "place" within them. I had some precedent for entertaining this enigmatic consideration.

Behind a deceptively located cattle gate opening onto a very different piece of land 1,000 miles to the south, first down an indeterminate drive, then down a featureless two-lane country blacktop, spreads a broad field surrounding a broken-down frame house with a stone chimney. Having driven up to the old farmhouse along a brushy dirt road, my grandfather would park the car near a windmill-fed cement cistern and honk the horn. Years of observing this ritual had taught me what to expect, and I would inevitably giggle at the sure approach of the cattle herd soon lumbering toward us in answer to the summons. If it was the right time of year, I would

Putting Down Roots | 25

slip over to the pomegranate tree that still survive͏ front window of the dilapidated house and pluck one o͏ red fruits for the universe of juicy bits inside. And ther͏ nd: juice staining my hands, rusty windmill blades creak͏ the breeze, expectant cattle congregating around the ing a treat, and family land stretching out around me ͏ eye could see.

My grandfather had been a cowboy on a south Texas ranch until the obligations of marriage convinced him to turn to more settled work. He became a merchant, ultimately owning the general mercantile store in downtown Berclair, 90 miles southeast of San Antonio. By the time I came along, the store was long-since gone and the town was little more than a post office and a Mexican cafe. But my grandparents remained in the white frame house one block off the highway with a spacious front porch and assorted chairs where they - and we - would enjoy the "cool" of the evening, chuckle at the re-telling of well-traveled memories, and wave at passing cars.

And there was, of course, the land. Grandad was, by no means, the largest landowner in the area – merely several hundred acres accumulated through a mixture of inheritance, strategic acquisition, and charitable purchase, contrasted with the several thousand acres held by some in the area. To a kid who had spent his years in city neighborhoods, however, the Diebel lands seemed vast and important. That even the cows obeyed him imbued my grandfather with an aura of reverence.

So I couldn't understand why that piece of his holdings protected behind a metal gate and giving sustenance to the tree bearing my pomegranates – the vast acreage that "we" had owned for longer than I had been alive – was always, without exception, referred to as "The Hartman Place."

"Why," I wondered, "isn't it called 'the Diebel Place'?"

The answer, as I have come to understand it, is at least two-fold – part explicit and part implied. The content of the former relates to my grandfather's sense of propriety. It simply struck him as offensively presumptuous to assert his own name. The latter is harder to name, but perhaps more important to acknowledge: the history of a place – its provenance, its sturdy trees and sweeping fields; the lives it has touched, the words and bird calls and animal steps now inhabiting its very soil; its story – is worth honoring. This land is too precious to treat as simply a clean page ready to capture whatever whim we might write upon it. The land has a narrative already underway. I never heard my grandfather speak such an insight, but the reverence with which he maintained not only the land, but its moniker, tells me he knew it and respected it. It was, he would rightly insist, "his," but only for a while, he would unflinchingly clarify. And the land - the place - had as much to teach as to receive.

Other teachers I have had, from disparate properties and places, have emphasized the same respectful discipline of paying close attention. Standing in the woods behind the cider mill and sugaring house, he and his family operate on the mountain in eastern Vermont where his ancestral family has been tapping trees and pressing apples for over 125 years, Willis Woods calls attention to the particularities of the trees.

> *You have to pay attention to each tree, because each one is different; different even from what it was last year. The undergrowth is different, the canopies above are different; one tree has been shaded while another has had full exposure to the sun. And then each year has its own weather patterns. Plus, you have to pay attention to where you tapped the tree last year so you don't tap this year in a way that will damage the tree. You just have to pay attention.*

A few miles away, Lisa Kaiman interacts with her 20 Jersey cows like they were her sisters. They have, as she describes it, "certain understandings." That much is clear. The cows answer not only to their names, but to their nicknames, and follow her gentle leadings regarding movements from pasture to milking room to feed troughs. Unhooking the last one from the milking equipment, she observes that each one of the cows is different. "They have personalities – and moods! In a commercial milking operation, the cows conform to the process. In my case, my process conforms to the cows and the moods they are in at the time. I have to pay close attention."

After watching the resident cheese maker and his visiting French consultant spend the morning laboring in the cheese house of Spring Brook Farm in Reading, Vermont, I mentioned that their cheese had been described to me as "high end" cheese. "What makes your cheese different from any of the brands I might find in the grocery store?" I asked. The two considered the question for several moments before the Frenchman finally answered, "In industrial cheese making, the milk conforms to the process. In artisanal cheese making, like you see here, our process conforms to the milk. The milk, after all, is different every day depending on whether the cows grazed in this field or that field," he said pointing out the windows. "It makes a difference whether they are grazing in April on that field or July in the same field. And then they have their moods, their health, and any given day's appetite. All of those factors – along with countless others – affect the character and quality of the milk they produce. So, we have to pay close attention."

On the opposite side of the country, Bill Sweat patiently tends the Oregon vineyard he and his wife Donna purchased in 2006. At *Winderlea*, the name they gave to the property and the wines that emerge from it, Bill and Donna adhere to bio-dynamic farming practices – an agricultural approach first developed in the early 1920s based on the spiritual insights and practical suggestions of the Austrian writer, educator and social activist Dr. Rudolf Steiner. Biodynamic farming is a controversial approach, given its planting schedule, guided by lunar phases, and its homeopathic preparations made from manure, minerals and herbs. Biodynamic farming is lampooned by many as so much "voodoo," while religiously adhered to by others. Sitting on the elevated patio overlooking the rows of vines, Bill – not nearly the wild-eyed fanatic that such practitioners are portrayed to be – talked with calm but sincere animation about his philosophy and particular application of such practices. When asked the inevitable question – "Does it work?" – he paused, looked affectionately over the vineyard, and finally answered, "Well, I don't finally know. But all that careful attention to even the most minute changes in the vineyard can't hurt, can it?"

These contemporary land stewards echo ancient wisdom. To the petulant complainer in the Book of Job, written perhaps in the 6th century BCE, God advises:

> *But ask the animals, and they will teach you; the birds of the air, and they will tell you; ask the plants of the earth, and they will teach you; and the fish of the sea will declare to you (12:7-8 NRSV).*

In his sweeping review of how the health of soil and civilizations is intertwined, David Montgomery recalls the counsel of Xenophon in the 4th century BCE who advised agents to:

> *Observe what their land could bear. "Before we commence the cultivation of the soil, we should notice what crops flourish best upon it; and we may even learn from the weeds it produces what it will best support." (David R. Montgomery, Dirt: The Erosion of Civilizations, Berkeley: University of California Press, 2007, p. 50.)*

"Like Xenophon," Montgomery goes on to report, "Roman agriculturalists understood that different things grew best in different soils; grapevines liked sandy soil, olive trees grew well on rocky ground." (Montgomery, p. 59)

Virgil, writing in the last century BCE, notes that:

*"Before we plow an unfamiliar patch*

*It is well to be informed about the winds,*

*About the variations in the sky,*

*The native traits and habits of the place,*

*What each locale permits, and what denies."*

ßß

As if echoing those words, the poet Alexander Pope counsels the listener, before attempting to impose one's own mark, to...

*"Consult the genius of the place in all;*

*That tells the waters or to rise, or fall;*

*Or helps th' ambitious hill the heav'ns to scale,*

*Or scoops in circling theatres the vale;*

*Calls in the country, catches opening glades,*

*Joins willing woods, and varies shades from shades,*

*Now breaks, or now directs, th' intending lines;*

*Paints as you plant, and, as you work, designs."*

(Alexander Pope 1688-1744, Epistles to Several Persons: Epistle IV
To Richard Boyle, Earl of Burlington)

Places, including the land we are looking for, have not been waiting, inertly, longing for our arrival. They have stories to tell, stories they will share with anyone who is attentive and listens.

This ancient wisdom brought depth and context to all the conversations I have had in the recent past, conversations with vegetable farmers and vineyard managers, with agronomists and ministers across the country. These people, who all treasure the land, have taught me the importance of paying attention to each place, letting it tell me how it needs to be cared for and what it is best able to grow. It ultimately has to do with flavor, but "flavor" as it is experienced not only literally but metaphorically as well.

As a clergy person, the conversations strike a familiar note. People in my profession have always had a kind of particularity in our relationship to God and God's creation. Some people are drawn to beaches and their undulating evocations of infinity, while others climb mountains and find themselves speechless at the panoramic vistas. Some, who feel an almost organic connection to farmland from which they draw identity and energy, are utterly mystified by the way others, standing in the midst of a frenetic city sidewalk, can be recharged by the pulsing urban "electricity." Places are particular, as are our connections to them.

Spirituality has long understood that linkage. Faithfulness, at its most evocative and transformational depth, is never about thinking lofty thoughts or closing one's eyes, gritting one's teeth and simply "believing." Trusting, yes. But that trust is never rooted, merely, in our minds' ability to wrap around one or any number of theological concepts about creation like so much pastry dough surrounding a sausage. Rather, it is about being present to the presence of God in real time and space, in the here and in the now. Hebrew scriptures claim that kind of particularity as the heart of Jewish understanding of their unique call as a people of God grounded in a particular place. Abram understood God's instruction, "not here." "Go to the place where I will lead you."

But God, the Israelites would discover, would not be confined to such binary alternatives. In fact, God just might pop up any place along the way and to anyone – even to a restless middle-aged couple on a farmstead in rural Warren County, Iowa.

In the biblical book of Genesis, a winsome but dubious character named Jacob, who would eventually become one of the patriarchs among his people, has a surprising dream out under the stars. He had created a few problems back home and is on his way to spend some time with relatives a safe distance away. With a stone for a pillow, he has a dream in which a ladder extends from the earth where he sleeps, upwards to heaven. Angels were making heavy traffic on that ladder, and in the midst of it all Jacob heard the voice of God say:

> *"The land on which you lie I will give to you and to your offspring;
> and your offspring shall be like the dust of the earth, and you shall
> spread abroad to the west and to the east and to the north and to
> the south; and all the families of the earth shall be blessed in you
> and in your offspring. Know that I am with you and will keep you
> wherever you go, and will bring you back to this land; for I will not*

*leave you until I have done what I have promised you." Then Jacob woke from his sleep and said, 'Surely the Lord is in this place – and I did not know it!' And he was afraid, and said, 'How awesome is this place! This is none other than the house of God, and this is the gate of heaven. (Genesis 28 NRSV)*

By settling among the grasses and trees, the stories and soil of the land we would eventually name "Taproot Garden," I was, in my own time and place and a thousand miles away from Berclair, the land of my ancestors, "channeling" the spirit of my grandfather. I reverently determined to pay that kind of precise attention by listening to and consulting the "genius of this place," so that I could come to "know" the holiness of this particular land we now called home.

ßß

# Chapter Four

# The Taste of This Place

*Find your hope, then, on the ground under your feet.*
*Your hope of Heaven, let it rest on the ground underfoot.*

Wendell Berry

Every place has its own personality. Every place has its own rhythm and dance and song. Every place, it turns out, sends forth a distinctive taste.

When Robert Drouhin, third generation of the venerable Burgundian wine-making family, purchased property near Dundee, Oregon, in 1987, it was as though a seal of approval had been stamped on the fledgling appellation in the Willamette Valley whose first grapevines had been in the ground less than two decades. Drouhin, however, already sensed what later Oregon winemakers would assert: "These hills were made for pinot noir." Sitting around a tasting table inside Domaine Drouhin's elegantly modern, gravity-fed facility affords an inquisitive visitor more than an appreciation of Robert's discerning vision. There, in addition to letting us sample Drouhin's Oregon bottling of pinot noir, the host pours samples of the family's Burgundian offerings as well. Experienced side-by-side, these wines, produced by the same family, by the same winemaker, from the same grape varietal, reveal themselves to be stunningly different. What accounts for the difference? The Drouhins' unequivocal answer is *terroir*.

*Terroir*, while not a word that most people use, has found a place at the center of my vocabulary. Never mind that it is French, nor that its primary use has been agricultural. Grape growers and winemakers have long spoken – in often misty-eyed tones – of the unique characteristics of specific hillsides and often tiny geographic regions called "climats." They have called attention to micro-climates – the characteristic rain patterns or prevailing breezes; the particular way the evening fog descends upon the vines, and the advantageous angle from which the sun dissipates it in the morning. They have noted the chemistry of the soil – whether acidic or alkaline, the minerals present, how well-drained or laden with clay it is. Certain areas, they have argued, are better than others – at least better for certain varietals. Place, they insist, imparts some flavor of itself into what is grown there. Terroir: the taste of place.

Amy Trubek, a culinary journalist writing not simply about ancient European winemaking philosophy but about the increasing use of the concept in American vegetable farming, acknowledges:

> *It is difficult to translate terroir from the French in a way that encapsulates all its meanings; in fact, some say terroir can never really be translated from the French at all. When it is attempted, the word is translated alternately as soil, locality, or part of the country. The French are unusual in the attention they place on the role of the natural world in the taste of food and drink. When the French take a bite of cheese or a sip of wine, they taste the earth: rock, grass, hillside, valley, plateau. They ingest nature, and this taste signifies pleasure, a desirable good. Gustatory pleasure and the*

*evocative possibilities of taste are intertwined in the French fidelity to the taste of place. (The Taste of Place: A Cultural Journey into Terroir,* by Amy B. Trubek, p. 9)

THE VENERABLE KENTUCKY FARMER/POET WENDELL BERRY, whose autograph and inspiration we had secured in that Kansas City visit, weighs in with his conviction that,

> *The most insistent and formidable concern of agriculture, wherever it is taken seriously, is the distinct individuality of every farm, every field on every farm, every farm family, and every creature on every farm. Farming becomes a high art when farmers know and respect in their work the distinct individuality of their place and the neighborhood of creatures that lives there. This has nothing to do with the set of personal excuses we call 'individualism' but is akin to the holy charity of the Gospels and the political courtesy of the Declaration of Independence and the Bill of Rights. Such practical respect is the true discipline of farming, and the farmer must maintain it through the muddles, mistakes, disappointments, and frustrations, as well as the satisfactions and exultations, of every actual year on an actual farm. (Imagination in Place,* Wendell Berry, p. 9)

When Brad Kessler and his wife purchased a Vermont farm and began to raise goats for cheese, they learned that:

> *Every raw-milk cheese is an artifact of the land; it carries the imprint of the earth from which it came. A cheese – even a fresh chèvre – is never just a thing to put in your mouth. It's a living piece of geography. A sense of place. Winemakers talk about the terroir of a particular wine, how a place's geology, drainage, soil, plants, and weather all contribute to a vintage. You can't create terroir artificially. It's the gift of a place, and what makes a pinot noir grown in one part of Burgundy taste different than one grown a kilometer*

*away – let alone the same grape raised in Australia. Terroir is the DNA of a place. It translates roughly as the "taste of the soil." (Goat Song: A Seasonal Life, A Short History of Herding, and the Art of Making Cheese, p. 159 )*

Others, of course, have tried their own definitional, translational hand at appropriating this almost mythical concept.

*Terroir is 40% climate, 40% soil, and 20% cultural. The cultural dimension involves the neighbors who can tell about the traditional fruits grown in the region and what farming methods have been shown to work.* (Al Courchesne, Frog Hollow Farm, California)

*Terroir is about more than just geography and climate; it is also about a sensibility, or even a spiritual quest. In making wine, the search is not to create the terroir but to discover the terroir. Really, you are learning to listen.* (Randall Grahm, Bonny Doon Vineyard)

Listening, then, and observing; and even tasting. All of a sudden, we had much to do as we offered ourselves into the arms of Taproot Garden. This, we would begin by comprehending, is a place like no other place. Winds would sweep through the trees and over the mounded prairie unlike anywhere else. Rains would fall and trickle over the land unlike anywhere else. We might plant Vidalia onion seeds in the garden but they would not taste the same as those grown in Vidalia, Georgia. Ours, along with everything else that grows here, would reflect its own terroir.

It all began to sound so monumental.

*I went to the woods because I wished to live deliberately, to front only the essential facts of life, and see if I could not learn what it had to teach, and not, when I came to die, discover that I had not lived. …I wanted to live deep and suck out all the marrow of life, to live so sturdily and Spartan-like as to put to rout all that was not life, to cut a broad swath and shave close, to drive life into a corner, and reduce it to its lowest terms, and, if it proved to be mean, why then to get the whole and genuine meanness of it, and publish its meanness to the world; or if it were sublime, to know it by experience.* (Henry David Thoreau, *Walden*)

Very shortly after moving to this farmstead we named it, for reasons as inscrutable then as now, "Taproot Garden." I don't know where the name came from. I wasn't even aware of the need to select a name. When one brings home a dog, a name becomes a pressing imperative; but never before had I considered a name for a new home. Nevertheless, the boxes were scarcely unpacked and the pictures hung on the walls before the name had emerged. We commissioned a graphic designer to create a logo, and not too long after taking possession of the finished art, we contracted with a sign maker for the entrance. The name, it seemed, had chosen us.

In some small way, like Thoreau before us, we had gone to the land because we, too, wished to live deliberately and deeply. I don't think we anticipated a lot of marrow sucking, but we were indeed intent on drawing from the wisdom of life's core. If a taproot reaches down into the depths of the soil to more solidly anchor whatever stems and leafs and fruits above, and to gather richer, more remote nutrition, then a taproot was precisely what we were after. Our move felt and continues to feel like one that brings the deeper nourishment closer to hand.

This is not to suggest that my prior vocational endeavor was artificial or fruitless. I am forever grateful for the calling, for the evocative mentors who helped me discern it, for the grandeur of its purpose and imagination, and for the people into whose proximity it drew me. But something about the execution of it always chaffed – the machinations, the protocols, the institutional expectations, the obligations both implied and stated. Like the teeth of transmission gears that never quite meshed, the operational and the vocational aspects of the work never quite found in me their rhythm.

This, of course, says far more about me than about the work. I have no real idea how the work should be done; I only know how I did it. To be sure, there were peers and role models that I watched and variously celebrated and derided. But I don't truly know what the practice of ministry was like for them. A wise teacher once noted that we are always comparing the "outside" of others with the "inside" of ourselves, and it's never a fair or accurate comparison.

All that, plus a certain inexorability about it. I recall a comment my brother made after returning with his family from the Macy's Thanksgiving Day Parade. Describing the incredible density of the crowd, he observed that you could almost pick up your feet and the crowd would carry you where it wanted you to go. My prior work had an element of that. For all its flexibility, ministry had a way of carrying me along in the directions it wanted me to go. And so, always swept along, I never quite felt capable of reconnecting with the pavement and initiating an alternative direction of my own within it.

Stepping, then, outside of it, we settled on the land. Deliberately. To "front only the essential facts of life, and to see if I could not learn what it had to teach." I wouldn't assert that it is the only way to do it – resettling onto a piece of land – but I suspect it's harder the farther away from the land we move. After all, the very word by which we call ourselves, "human," is rooted in the Latin word, "humus." We are deeply connected to the land. The ancient Hebrews understood this. The word they used to name the first human, Adam, literally means "of the earth." Dirt creature. Dirt, then, in our distant past and in our brand new future.

ßß

# Chapter Five

# A Deeper Dig

*You shall eat your fill and bless the L*ORD* your God*
*for the good land that he has given you.*

Deuteronomy 8:10 (NRSV)

Horticulturally, a taproot creates an anchoring center from which other, more lateral roots may sprout. A germinating seed sends down a stabilizing leg on which to stand. It reaches deep, down into the kind of sustaining nourishment not found closer to the surface. Once extended and firmly, securely in place, the taproot sends out feelers to explore the adjacent space. That's something of the way we understood our move to the country. Which is to acknowledge that at some inarticulate level, we hoped for more than simply an outdoor classroom in which to learn about vegetables. In ways for which we had no words, we came in search of a deeper, more anchoring sensibility about the movements of nature, the alchemy of nourishment, and our particular role in the wonder of it all.

Feeling light-headed amidst the flame, flash, and fizz of contemporary digitized and over-marketed culture, we hoped to tap into something older and wiser and ultimately more sustainable. It wasn't to escape, but to somehow enter the world more fully. Hence, this deeply appropriate name for our new home: "Taproot Garden," a place intended not simply for living, but for cultivating new insights into how it is that we are – and continue to be – alive.

After unpacking everything we needed to live, we started looking around the property with a sense of glorious but paralyzing awe. There is something intimidating about a blank page. Complete openness. Perfect opportunity. But there are no lines, no givens, no parameters within which to narrow choices. Anything is possible, and, therefore, everything is on the table. It wasn't the wide open expanse of possibility onto which God looked out in the beginning of all things according to the Bible's account in the book of Genesis – that messy chaos and void that the Hebrews knew poetically as "tohu-wa-vohu"; there were, after all, trees already growing here, deer already roaming, grass waving in the breeze, and bluebirds and butterflies fluttering through.

We weren't even the first humans to settle here. As the days grew shorter with winter's approach and the temperatures started to fall, we settled into the slower and more interior work of the season. I retrieved from the stowed stack of real estate documents the Abstract we had been warned, under penalty of certain cataclysm, never to lose. Not that it would be easy to lose. Thick, with pages too oversized to fit neatly into a file, the Abstract dominates whatever closet or corner or box to which it is relegated like an overweight Saint Bernard. But not nearly as lovable as a dog. It is every bit the drab, imposing, almost mathematical document it presents itself to be, laced with dates and abbreviations and the usual dizzying fog of legal jargon. But buried within the successive transitions, recounted in drone-like succession, is a fanciful window into the story of this place.

It begins in August of 1853 with the legal transfer of NE 1/4 SE 1/4 Sec. 22, Twp. 77 N., Range 24 West 5th by the United States to David Colclazier. Fascinated, I contacted our realtor and asked, "Who owned the property prior to 1853?"

"Indians?" he mused.

True, I was eventually to learn, but the story is more textured than that.

Indigenous peoples did, indeed, call these acres home, along with the whole of Iowa. County names and towns, rivers and landmarks still bear the names of tribes and chiefs and descriptive references. French explorers criss-crossed the area for decades, claiming the region for France until 1763. I've found no mention of how those already living here at the time of those explorations felt about that claim. I hope they didn't get too attached to this asserted French identity, because in 1763 Spain obtained title to the region as a spoil of war; that is, until 1800 when they signed it back over to France. The ink on the transfer, however, was hardly dry before France ceded it to the United States in consideration of $15,000,000 in cash and other benefits. Lewis and Clark passed nearby in their expedition of 1803. Who knows how many others? The identity of what is now known as Iowa languished until June 12, 1838 when, by act of Congress, the "Territory of Iowa" was constituted. Statehood would follow in 1846.

Of course, all of these transfers and recognitions were only real on paper. They had nothing to do with the actual residence and concourse of those indigenous people who actually lived here and held their own legal title to the land by various treaties. Beginning in the 1820s a succession of treaties were negotiated on behalf of the United States government and various tribes, including the Sac and Fox, the Chippewa, the Winnebago, Ottawa, and Pottawatta-mie tribes, opening up the lands of Iowa to settlement by newcomers. Closer to home, the area known as Warren County – including that parcel eventually to be known as Taproot Garden – was, as one source describes it, "gained from the Indians, not by a bloody conquest but by peaceful negotiation" (*History of Warren County,* Des Moines: Union Historical Company, 1879).

Included in the tract of land that the Sac and Fox Indians ceded to the United States Government in the treaty of October 11, 1842, Warren County came to its new settlers bearing the fingerprints of Indian Chiefs Keokuk, Appanoose, Poweshiek, and Panassa. Settlement was approved to begin May 1, 1843. "It is to this treaty," opines the History of Warren County, "that the present citizens and property owners of Warren County… are indebted, in a great measure, for their comfortable homes, their fertile fields, and their valuable estates in this 'beautiful land.'"

They cohabited "quietly and peacefully," native peoples and white settlers, from the spring of 1843 until the fall of 1845 until, by prior agreement, the new settlers would assume full control and occupancy. The native peoples who had stewarded this land moved on to designated land southwest of Kansas City.

People moved in and out, settled and built, hunted and farmed. A few more years passed until that momentous day when the afore referenced Mr. David Colclazier signed on the dotted line and became the first named owner of this property. Over the succeeding years, the land would be variously sold to Mr. Miles White in 1855, and by A.W. Brandon and his wife Bertha to G.E. Sherriff in 1902. Martha Tuttle inherited the land in 1912. George Sherriff would reenter the picture in 1957 in an "Affidavit of Possession" in which C.K. Bierma swears to the public:

*Am personally acquainted with George E. Sherriff the present owner, and know that he is in actual possession of said land, and that he and his predecessors in the chain of possession of said premises, have since prior to January 1, 1940 been in the continuous, actual, visible, open, notorious, exclusive and hostile adverse possession thereof under color of title and claim of right as against all the world, and have farmed, cultivated and improved said land, either personally or through tenants claiming under them, and have paid the taxes thereon, and that neither the title nor the right to possession of said present owner, or of those under whom he claims, has been disputed or openly attacked by anyone."*

I can only imagine what all that means, though it certainly sounds interesting. Whatever else its impact, the Affidavit paved the way for selling the property to John and Janell Hines on contract. It would not be a happy residence. John would eventually relocate to Idaho, ostensibly to secure better wages. It turns out that what he secured was another wife… before he had legally quitted his first. Legal tussles ensued until a satisfactory division was granted in 1963. All this is in the Abstract – in even juicier detail. It's really quite scandalous, but I'll leave all that to the reader's imagination. The land would subsequently be sold again, divided and parceled, and eventually be known as the Nelson Subdivision; and later still, according to the sign at the entrance, "Taproot Garden."

In other words, we are not the first to be here, neither flora nor fauna. We cannot name all who have been here, nor can we chronicle all that has happened here. But viscerally we knew that whatever happened next on this fragment of landscape to which we now held the deed would, in some way, involve us. And no, it wasn't primordial chaos, but it was **our** chaos, and the responsibility of imprinting some particular order is no small stewardship.

The process, then, would begin by making choices; but according to what?

That is the wonder of creating a garden.

If, as in our case, one doesn't intend to cultivate it all, which *particular section* will be – and why? Surely drainage issues would be one factor. Proximity may well be another. Access to water quickly emerges as a priority, as does openness to sun. And how big? What is the "enough" beyond which enough becomes "too much"?

We had added rain barrels to harvest rainwater off the garden shed out back, and so these water sources became the anchor of the southwest corner. A more careful examination of the field revealed a juvenile oak tree that could serve as the southeasterly point. A few years down the road, assuming the tree's continuing growth, we will need to shift the space away from its shade, but for now it won't interfere. Stepping off a comparable distant north from both points suggested a rough 60' X 60' outline.

The U.S. Geological Soil Survey indicates that the land is mostly Ladoga Silt Loam, but exactly what that means I have yet to comprehend. It isn't the finest soil around, but a knowledgeable friend reassures me that it isn't the worst.

I mowed out the short field grass covering the garden plot, and then prepared the soil for springtime by enriching it with compost and manure and a few other organic tricks I had been reading about, finishing just as the first shivers of winter drifted through.

The garden, I recognized, would never be more perfect than it was at precisely that moment – fertile and productive and safe within the confines of my imagination. But we didn't move out here to enjoy an imaginary garden, and so the dirty but gloriously evocative work began: the great and patient alchemy of soil and worm, rain and sun, seed and weed and hoe and – with any luck – harvest.

One could justifiably say that it was an odd time to take up gardening full-time – autumn, when everything is winding down in anticipation of winter. To be sure, there were projects to complete – a greenhouse to build, fruit trees to plant, a garden plot to demarcate – but there was precious little "gardening" to do. Once the greenhouse was assembled through the ministrations of Larry and Shirley, our generous and more mechanically minded friends, I established some greens and herbs in trays for growing in that protected space, and they required daily tending – watering, examining, offering some encouraging words – but those essential demands consumed little time. The tools were stowed, the rain barrels were emptied and stored, the hoses were wound and deposited in the shed.

Horticulturally speaking, we had entered the slow time. The land quiets, and there is little for this entering farmer to do but walk around, noticing the grasses, peering through the brush opened by now-naked branches, seeing what only weeks ago was obscured. The trees looked different, stripped of their imposing wardrobe – vulnerable in a way that is true of any living thing. The grasses, so recently upright and undulating in the wind like a dry land ocean, now lay prone as if hibernating for the winter – which, I suppose, is precisely true. The lawn that seemed hopelessly carpeted by fallen walnuts and hedge apples had been largely cleared by the squirrels – or whatever. Brittle branches, broken by wind and the weight of an early snow in the prior weeks, littered the pathways and called for attention.

I could only imagine what was happening beneath the surface. Do the worms and microbes press deeper as the soil hardens with the freezing? Do the roots essentially take a deep breath and hold it for the next four months? To this day such details are beyond my reach. I am confined to monitoring what happens in plainer view – the deer, a herd of does, a couple of adolescent fawns, and only occasionally the more reticent buck, venturing out into the open field for food; the rabbits, hidden in the grass in plain sight, jumping away from the step of my foot; the occasional cardinal on a branch, searching for food or interests more romantic.

There is little to do but walk around. And pay attention. But surely that is important – essential and even reverential – work; seeing, watching, hearing, noticing. This is the time to get acquainted, intimately, with this place that has already become, in an anticipatory way, my teacher; and I dare not neglect my studies.

In other words, this would be my book work in this quietly encompassing classroom of the fallow field.

ßß

Christmas Day arrived a short three months into our residency, and that afternoon we pushed our way a little farther into the brush toward the back of the property. It was a spontaneous expedition mounted primarily to get Tir, our beloved Welsh Corgi, a little exercise out of the house. We navigated the paths to the southeast of the house, waving at the alpacas grazing across the way on the property next door, and then headed north around and behind the garden site. We spoke little; such words that were uttered voiced our appreciative amazement that on Christmas Day the weather still permitted such excursions. The sky was blue, the temperature brisk but mild for the season, and the wonder of the nativity still full within us.

The mowed path led us alongside the field grass dome, back to where the landscape begins to descend toward the spring. Trees, and the underbrush that almost webs them together, here create a natural fence line that I had only breached once – and Lori, never.

She pushed on, brushing back and breaking off intruding twigs and branches. I picked my way more cautiously, reticent to snag the sweater I still wore from church that morning. Realizing her curiosity had been blunted by the impeding thicket, Lori turned back. Then I, promising to gas up the power trimmer one of these days and clear the entanglement away, followed her lead.

Noting that the grasses had thinned for the winter, we, like the magi, returned home by a different way – off the cleared path, through the field and along the western edge of the property. Deer paths, we could discern, created a criss-crossing highway system of comings and goings, and we stumbled across more than a few deer-sized matted places where it has apparently been common for them to bed down for the night.

The welcoming land cradled us on our bucolic stroll, content to make room for us to put down our roots here. Someday, I would eventually get busy with that power trimmer, though I admitted to some reticence. It wasn't so much laziness or my clumsiness working with that intimidating device as it was a sense of humble deference and respect. It seemed presumptuous, after all, to scarcely get unpacked before whacking away at what we had found here, imposing our particular vision of how this place should be before we had so much as listened and sought to understand its own. Our own fingerprints, we knew, would eventually be felt here – we would participate in the shaping and the nurturing and, to be sure, the trimming – but for a while we would walk, trace, observe the movement of the winds and the patterns of the animals, the bending of the grasses, the sentry points of the evergreens, and the squirrels' disposition of the fallen nuts and hedge apples.

If ours was to be a relationship with this land of participation rather than imposition, we had much to hear,

and see,

and touch,

and taste,

and learn.

# Chapter Six

# Learning to Love the Soil

*In every handful of healthy soil, there are more organisms than the number of people who have ever lived on Planet Earth.*

Dr. Kristine Nichols, in *Kiss the Ground*, p. 137

It is likely clear by this time that the "great outdoors" has, for the largest share of my life, had more to do with viewing pleasure than active engagement. Count me among its grateful admirers – the rolling ocean waves, the mountain vistas, the wooded streams – but those natural wonders have had everything to do with appreciative wonder and very little to do with real involvement. I enjoy the feel of beach sand between my toes as much as the next guy, and hiking through a forest path, but I have accumulated paltry knowledge of oceanography or the intricacies of sylvan flora or fauna. The closest I came to "agriculture," growing up, was mowing yards; and that had more to do with economics than "nature." Although economically speaking, I was grateful that grass had this persistent knack for growing.

I could argue that, growing up in the blistering heat of west Texas, spending much time outdoors wasn't good for my health. But the high temperatures didn't keep me off the tennis courts or any number of other outdoor pursuits of interest I could choose to fill a few hours of time. But I can hardly compare myself to farmers and ranchers in Texas who spend the better part of their days out among the elements. The simple reality was that my interests largely occupied me indoors. I played the guitar – most commonly sitting on the edge of my bed. I played the piano, I read books, I participated in school plays and the school choir and speech team and hung out with my friends, either indoors or in a car heading from one indoor activity to another. There were summer boat outings to water ski, and the occasional cookout at summer camp, but file these under "social activities" rather than "considered reflection."

Once on a church youth group trip we stopped at the Grand Canyon while en route to our planned destination. I have this embarrassing memory of standing at the rim, surveying the immensity of it all – the natural spectacle of the river-ripped chasm laying bare the very bowels of the earth thousands of feet below me – and, after a few minutes, looking at my watch wondering aloud if we shouldn't be loading back into our vehicles and continuing down the road. I was probably 16 years old, impatient, and so invested in my delusion of autonomy as to have no visceral capacity for comprehending how tiny I was.

Dirt has never found its way, much, under my fingernails. I've scrubbed off plenty of newspaper ink smudges from my fingertips, but dirt has never been a problem. Into adulthood my time has been spent in an office, in hospital rooms, meeting rooms and worship spaces where the only plants were potted artificials. I tilled ideas, and words were the seeds I sowed. "Dirt" was what you washed from your hands, cleaned from your food, swept from the floor, and kicked from your shoes.

And then we wound up here – inexplicably, given my history – on these ten acres of Taproot Garden, learning from scratch about seed propagation, plant cultivation, fruit and nut trees, and the interplay of sun and rain.

And soil.

I should have commenced this adventure with a higher geological theology. Dirt, after all, factors significantly in our formation. Others have different memories of origin and different stories by which to share them. An ancient Norse creation myth kicks it off with the melting of a frozen river to form the primeval giant and his accompanying cow. While the giant slept, his underarm sweat begat two frost giants, one male and one female. An African account of creation introduces humankind as the vomit of the deity. Nice. A Navajo version traces our ancestors through the "first people" from earlier worlds – animals and insects that resulted from the meeting of various clouds. For J. R. R. Tolkien in *The Silmarillion*, creation was an act of musical harmony and discord.

In contrast to those wonderfully evocative stories, the biblical book of Genesis focuses on its own intriguing medium, one that is less poetic than music, less ethereal than the clouds, significantly drier than rivers, but only slightly more noble than vomit. Dirt. That, according to the text, is the nature of us. Soil. We've been trying to make sense of that ever since.

"Then the LORD God formed a creature from the dust of the ground and breathed into its nostrils the breath of life, and the creature became a living being" (Genesis 2:7 NRSV).

From the humus, a human. Animated soil. Somehow, mysteriously, made in the very image of its creator. Exactly what we are to make of that affirmation is unclear, although my comprehension of God has often felt muddy to me. But from the very beginning, apparently, scholars have debated about this dirt-born image. Is it an intrinsic tug toward humility, a word which also comes from the word "humus" ("remember, you are nothing but dirt"), or is it a nod to an attribute fundamentally holy?

Both, I suppose, are useful, but I confess that I lean more in the direction of holiness. Whatever we are to make of the earth, it is clear from the story that God went to great pains to set it apart; and I rather like the picture of God artistically – or is it playfully – fashioning me out of clay and thereby leaving all over my being fingerprints of the divine. Perhaps that helps account for my fascination these days with soil – honoring it, understanding its particular attributes, tending it, and stewarding out of its depths food that nourishes me even as it was first nourished by the worms and the minerals and the myriad constituent parts of the land that is – or at least will be – our garden.

My land. The land that is me. Holiness, indeed.

Early on, then, our education turned to dirt – that inert matrix into which, as far as I knew, one pushes seed. Our first planting season I assumed that, once the ground was cleared and tilled, all I had to do was decide what seeds went where, scatter them thusly, cover and keep watered, along with occasional weeding. That characterization would prove to be the first of many ignorances I would need to overcome. Weeding, I quickly learned, would necessarily beg my attentions more than occasionally. Watering – how often, how much – proved to be more voodoo than discipline. Tilling, I've since learned, can create more problems than it solves. And as for the dirt, itself, it's hard to know where to begin.

There is a difference between dirt and soil. That was news to me, but knowledge has a way of forcing its way in. Dirt, I soon discovered, doesn't occasion much growth. Dirt is merely the granular detritus of rocks and fossilized materials. It is, indeed, inert. Soil, by contrast – the stuff of which gardens are made – is teeming with life. It is the almost mystical aggregation of dirt, microbial activity, mycorrhizal fungi, organic material, moisture and space in which life resides and is nourished. No one can possibly count them all, but as the claim cited at the beginning of this chapter asserts, there are more living things beneath the surface of the soil than above it. Though we tend to view it as merely that ubiquitous "stuff" that is forever out there and under foot, soil is better thought of as an organism itself, requiring the same tender loving care as any other life form. It needs food and water, nutritional replenishment and nurture. Repeatedly, as I pursued my new education, I came across the counsel to "feed the soil, not the plant." The soil, the wisdom goes, knows better how to feed the plant than I ever will.

Our education was slow but is progressing along. Eschewing chemical enhancements and poisonous preventions – the modern steroids of agricultural life – we had to learn patience with the natural cycles of life and death and the decay that necessarily turns dirt into soil; death back into life. Unlike life as I had come to know it, burdened by dumpsters of weekly collected refuse, nature knows no waste. Dropped leaves, spent vines, excrement, and the collected bedding from the chicken coops are systematically recycled and rehabilitated into fertility and new life.

It is quite miraculous, really; a scrambling of all my old clarities of trash and treasure that has shifted the way I think of everything, even the unrelated. Now when I throw something away, it is with a sense of shame that I haven't been creative enough – imaginative enough – to conceive of how that little or large bit of refuse could find its next use as the raw material giving birth to something new. That, after all, is how nature works – in a circle rather than a straight line. There are no casualties. Only new beginnings. Who knows, one of these days it may successfully recycle me into a real farmer.

So, what exactly had we purchased? What was this soil we intended to cultivate?

Without getting too deeply into the weeds (there are enough of those anyway) there are two ways to find answers to those questions. The simplest is to consult the Natural Resources Conservation Service – what was once known as the "Soil Conservation Service," which I would eventually discover had some connection to my history. The NRCS maintains soil survey maps of virtually everywhere in the United States – satellite maps, topographical maps, and of course soil maps. It's a little scary to me how they have come to know these things in such intimate detail, but they are the government and they are here to help. Ahem. One simply provides an address or a designated "Area of Interest" and the NRCS can load you down with all kinds of information. With a little bit of technological savvy, much of this information can now be accessed online.

The other, more involved way of gleaning more specific data about a property is to extract a soil sample from that "Area of Interest" that is subsequently analyzed by a qualified lab. There are detailed instructions for obtaining such a sample. Though a shovel is acceptable, the preferred tool is a long, tube-like instrument with a handle on top. The tube is inserted a foot or so into the ground, and then withdrawn now bearing a cylindrical core sample of soil which is discharged into a bucket. Multiple such plugs are taken from various locations around the target area, deposited into the bucket and ultimately mixed. A baggy full of the resulting concoction is then sent to the lab for testing.

I performed this sampling a year into our residence at Taproot Garden, at the close of our first gardening season, borrowing the tool from the local office of the USDA Extension Service. Like a sadistic surgeon I stabbed and cored all over the garden, biopsying the cultivational body. After stirring the accumulation, I scooped a representative sample into a bag and entrusted it to the mail. Some unfortunate soul at Iowa State University – a beleaguered grad-student, I suspect – subjected the sample to all the whirs and lights and highly technical gizmos and gadgets of the laboratory, which almost certainly included microscopes and beakers, and returned to me a report in a matter of weeks.

So, what was the verdict? Meh. Let's just say the report wasn't the agricultural equivalent of a blue-ribbon, nor was it leaked to farmers who anxiously formed a long line outside of our door begging for the opportunity to cultivate it. It is OK, but not great. As I mentioned in the previous chapter, the technical description is "Ladoga silt loam," moderately well drained. There is an adequate layer of topsoil, which is good, with a parent material of loess. That latter refers to wind-deposited dust – part silt, part sand, part clay – that over the eons has settled and become loosely held in place by calcium carbonate. Loess, generally speaking, has challenges, mostly in its vulnerability to erosion. The very same wind that deposited it can pick it back up again. And rain has very little trouble washing it away.

All of those challenges apply to Taproot Garden. According to our soil analysis, our "Land Capability Classification" is 3e, indicating "severe limitations that restrict the choice of plants or that require special conservation practices or both," primarily due to the erodibility. The garden is planted on 5 to 9 percent slopes.

But, of course, we are up for challenges – especially when we don't know what we are doing. We forged ahead, now armed with a wealth of information of dubious value, built as it was on a vocabulary utterly foreign to us. There are books for that, however, and so, we leaned into our ongoing education.

Who, after all, wouldn't want to learn all they could about Ladoga silt loam?

# Chapter Seven

# Connecting with the Spirit
## of Walter Lowdermilk

*These are things we learned from our ancestors,*
*and we will tell them to the next generation.*

Psalm 78:3-4 (CEV)

Once upon a time my mother loaned me a book, presumably with the intention that I read it.

Right away.

I didn't – at least not for a long time. For maybe a decade the book languished on a remote shelf in my office. Nothing about the book invited attention. Clearly self-published at a time when the tools to accomplish such an undertaking were crude, it had a typical paperback cover, and it was bound and glued like a "real" book, but the pages looked typed and mimeographed and unappealing. On the back cover was a grainy, black and white photograph of a severe looking woman – the author and wife of a distant relative whose life story held no prima facia appeal. When I say "distant" I mean he is a triple back-flip gainer uncle, thrice removed. Or something like that. More technically, as closely as I can work it out, he and my grandmother share a grandfather, which makes us first cousins twice removed. I think. So, not close. Let's just say that I didn't jump right on the book.

And then, after all those years, my mother found her own renewed interest in the subject and asked that I return the volume. Praying it still might reside where last I had seen it, I gratefully retrieved it and hastily – guiltily – began to read in case the subject ever came up in family conversation. Immediately I was transfixed, beginning with the epigraph – what that relative had famously referred to as the 11th Commandment :

> *Thou shalt inherit the holy earth as a faithful steward, conserving its resources and productivity from generation to generation. Thou shalt safeguard thy fields from soil erosion, thy living waters from drying up, thy forests from desolation, and protect thy hills from overgrazing by the herds, that thy descendants may have, abundance forever. If any shall fail in this stewardship of the land, thy fruitful fields shall become sterile, stony ground and wasting gullies; and thy descendants shall decrease and live in poverty or perish from off the face of the earth.*

With every page turned I discovered, much to my surprise, an inspiration and something of a soul mate. The book, written by Inez Marks Lowdermilk, recounts the story of her life with Walter Clay Lowdermilk – her husband and my albeit distant relative, beginning in the early 1900's and continuing through his death in 1974.

Walter, I discovered, was a Rhodes Scholar and an early soil conservationist who worked with the Chinese government until beating a hasty departure just in front of the communist takeover. After he and Inez retreated to the States, he was recruited by Franklin Roosevelt to join the federal government and the U.S.

Department of Agriculture under Henry Wallace to help create what became the U.S. Soil Conservation Service. It was in that capacity that he was sent on an 18-month research mission in Europe, the Middle East, and Africa to study land use practices since the time of the Romans.

When he and Inez eventually arrived in Palestine in 1938, he was aghast. A devout Methodist layman, he had been reared on the stories of Canaan and the abundant land flowing with milk and honey described in the pages of the Hebrew scriptures. There, according to the books of Exodus and Numbers, Israelite scouts surveyed the Promised Land before crossing the river to take it. Reporting back to their leaders the discovery of a land so fertile it produced grapes so large that "a single cluster had to be carried on a pole between them."

But instead of this plentiful land of milk and honey, what Lowdermilk found was a wasteland – a desolate wilderness taxed beyond any useful service, barely able to support the scattered population that called the region home. What had happened? Why was the imagery of the Bible at such a disconnect with what he was seeing with his own eyes? Not surprisingly, the British government, in control of the area at the time, had forbidden any further settlement in the area – even by a ship load of Jewish refugees who sailed into port while the Lowdermilks were visiting, desperately fleeing Nazism in Europe.

Moved and troubled, Lowdermilk began to survey the region – or, as he put it, reading what the soil itself had written in the land. And what he discerned was that the land wasn't useless; it was simply exhausted – abused and overused. What was needed, he argued, was not abandonment, but reclamation. The soil, he knew, could erupt into blossom again. And after the founding of the new State of Israel in the wake of World War 2, he returned at the invitation of the nascent Israeli government to work on soil erosion prevention and the reclamation of that biblical fertility. As a result of that work, he came to be known in Israel as "the father of the Israel water plan" that resulted in thousands of miles of contour terraces designed for erosion prevention. One of his enduring legacies there is the Lowdermilk School of Agricultural Engineering at the Israel Institute of Technology in Haifa.

There is a lot to be proud of in his story. Since that long-overdue and obligatory read, I have purchased and given away as many used copies of that forlorn book as I could locate online, along with worn copies of the various books he published in the course of his work. Walter has become a source of personal pride and principled admiration. And did I mention that we are related? Several recent books on soil management and the history of conservation devote whole chapters to the work and legacy of this now-claimed and celebrated relative. And in the spring of 2018 the Israeli government included him in their list of 70 Americans most responsible for the establishment of Israel, alongside luminaries like President Harry Truman and former Secretary of State George Schultz. After enumerating his contributions, the citation concluded, "In appreciation of his many contributions to the Jewish state, Israel Minister of Development Mordecai Bentov put it best: 'We don't need powdered milk. We need Lowdermilk.'"

Predating my own commitment by many decades, Lowdermilk had forged this relationship with the land. *The New York Times* obituary announcing his death and remembering his life repeated his warning that humankind "could destroy the basis of the food supply and culture by failing to meet the responsibility to preserve natural resources."

"Civilization," the *Times* obituary quoted him as saying, "is running a race with famine, and the outcome is still in doubt."

It became Lowdermilk's life work to teach the world that it isn't only people who get bullied and abused and tortured and left to languish in despair. The very land around us – once loose and loamy and teaming with life – wears bruises of its own in the grayish, hard-packed powder leached of any signs of life.

Walking the trails around Taproot Garden's 3-acre prairie, spreading manure in the garden and planting seeds in the fertile soil, I think again of the serious attention there is to pay, and fresh respect to offer to this basic and sustaining gift beneath our very feet. Walter Lowdermilk's "11th Commandment" got it right: if our descendants are to enjoy the earth's abundance we have to live today as its faithful stewards. Absent that care, they shall indeed "decrease and live in poverty or perish from off the face of the earth."

It is rather embarrassing that it took me this long to realize it.

What else, I began to wonder, is "out there" just waiting for me to realize it?

CHAPTER EIGHT

# EARLY TURNINGS

*A sower went out to sow. And as he sowed, some seed fell on the path...Other seed fell on rocky ground... Other seed fell among thorns...Other seed fell into good soil and brought forth grain, growing up and increasing and yielding thirty and sixty and a hundredfold.*

Mark 4:3-8 (NRSV)

On the occasion of our first wedding anniversary, Lori and I returned to Vermont where we had honeymooned the year before. On that now-long ago trip we didn't retrace exactly the same ground of that earlier visit, but we did return to the small community of Waitsfield where we had serendipitously met the granddaughter of Maria von Trapp of *The Sound of Music* fame, Elisabeth von Trapp and her husband. Waitsfield is one of the quintessential Vermont villages that had aesthetically insisted that we park and walk around as we were driving through the year before. On this second trip we stopped again and went into Kenyon's Store, one of those general purpose variety/farm/ranch/hardware stores that are, to us, hypnotic. One of the souvenirs I couldn't resist was a black and red checked wool jacket. OK, and yes, I also bought the matching cap with ear flaps. For the record, I am the only one in the family who holds them special.

The purchase, however, proved to be prescient. Some days on the farm cry out for the Vermont wool and this particular day was one of them. During the night temperatures had fallen to 16 degrees, holding in place the dusting of snow that had fallen earlier in the afternoon. Forecasted to reach 40 degrees, morning broke full of brisk sunshine. And frost. Since the following day was supposed to bestow upon us steady rains, followed by snow through the night, this day, of course, was the day necessary for planting the garlic.

The prior week, after clearing the Thanksgiving table, brother-in-law Steve filled a bag of cloves from his own supply for us to use in our first garden season. Unlike me, Steve knows what he is doing – planting and actually harvesting an ample supply each year to extend through the winter. So, when he assured me it wasn't too late to get the garlic cloves into the ground, I gratefully accepted the gift with good intentions. Now a week later and very possibly too late, I was running up against the calendar wall. It was now or never, regardless of the temperatures in the teens, snow on the ground, and my general ignorance on the subject (beyond Steve's cursory coaching).

Pulling on my thermal underwear, the fleece lined corduroy shirt, the Carhartt bib overalls given to me as a parting gift by the church, and my beloved Vermont wool jacket, I headed out to the garden with Tir, a shovel and the garlic. I chose an area just inside the intended enclosure, just beyond the beaten path worn by the movement of deer. Taking a deep breath and preparing for a fight, I heaved my energies into the shovel.

The truth is I received better than I deserved. The ground, despite the icy temperatures, was actually quite willing and receptive, turning over with little effort. The wriggling earthworms whose hidden home I had so violently shoveled gave me some optimism that the bulbs and subsequent seeds that would be joining them in this soil would find a habitable space.

I dug the trench to what I hoped was an appropriate depth, lodged the cloves along the bottom evenly spaced, retrieved the ones that Tir had pirated and sampled (not knowing whether his teeth indentations had killed the bulb), and planted them together at the end of the row. And, gently replaced and tamped down the soil. Mulching matter from my autumn efforts completed the cov-

ering. And then – as with vir-
tually everything related to this
project – I reconciled myself to
the wait. And prayed – that the
garlic would actually mature
into the marinara, minestro-
ne soup, and Mexican salsa of
which we were dreaming.

ßß

And that Tir's breath – curiously pungent as he licked my face – would return to normal. For the moment, he smelled more Italian than Welsh.

The garlic, of course, was our first down-payment on the garden-to-be. More specimens would crowd the spaces alongside the pungent bulbs. As winter settled in, long months removed from spring planting, we had the luxury of anticipating.

The dangerous joy of a gardener's winter – especially a gardener whose optimism and imagination far out-pace his knowledge and experience – is getting lost under the flutter of seed catalogs newly descending as the new year approached. "New this season" joins with "perennial favorite" to entice one indulgence after another. Over the weekend, I three times clicked on the "checkout now" button of the seed companies' online catalog sites; heirlooms, open-pollinated, and all manner of saved seeds, from the familiar asparagus ("Purple Passion" and "Jersey Supreme") and beans ("Taylor Strain", "Black Jet") and Brussels sprouts ("Nautic"), to the ever curious kohlrabi ("Korridor" and "Azur Star"), the thematically obligatory rutabaga ("American Purple Top"), the reliable Swiss chard ("Fordhook Giant" and "Bright Lights"), and the essential peppers, squashes, tomatillos, and tomatoes (too many varieties to count). I even managed to find seeds for the Padron peppers we had enjoyed as an appetizer at a restaurant in Napa Valley.

I say "*dangerous* joy" because the "joy" part of the phrase can get expensive. Sure, the packets of seed aren't much – from around $3 to just over $5 – but, alas, it adds up. Like pushing your tray through a cafeteria line where everything looks good, and you came hungry. I put some novelties on my tray (like the striped Asian eggplant, the Christmas lima beans, egg yolk tomato, and the round tomato-shaped pimento) along with some aesthetics (like the zinnias and strawflowers). A Texas gardener wouldn't want to try and make it through without a couple varieties of okra and a good stand of collard greens. I could already taste the poblanos and anchos, and my mouth watered in anticipation of a softball-sized Brandywine tomato. All of which is to say that my purchases were broad and deep. But, hey, they are seeds – the promise of things to come!

Lest you think I had repressed all realism, I was well aware that my garden would never be more prolific than it was in my imagination, right then, before a single seed had been sown. I did understand that it would require a labor-intensive risk to actually go through with the project. It's easy, after all, to talk about it – grandly, sweepingly, philosophically, nobly. It gets dirtier, sweatier, and more exhausting from that point forward.

And yet, we came to Taproot for this. In fact, it was almost redundant to order seeds for this place where everything about this endeavor had to do with seeds already planted. Dreams, imagination, lives, spirit – seeds of a very different variety carefully and naïvely palmed and carried to this new beginning and thumbed into what already felt like fertile soil – at least for the soul's prosperity. With all of this abundance, why not a few hundred seeds more?

ONCE THE SEEDS HAVE BEEN ORDERED, it doesn't take long for them to arrive, clogging the mailbox with the possibility of growth and harvest, dreams of swelling tomatoes and hanging peppers above ground and fattening carrots and beets below the surface. The mail carrier quickly learned our names and our intentions, delivering a steady stream of the bloated packages. I brought them inside and piled the packets on the dining room table, experimenting with various organizational strategies. Mostly, however, I just absorbed the reality of them. Each day I retrieved the box of seed packets and fanned through the varieties, fingering the photos of the intentions inside and imagining them popping up in my garden. It became almost an obsession. Still the depths of winter and already I was harvesting a crop in my mind. A "bumper crop," I'll add, although I routinely allowed room for a shriveled potato or two and some undeveloped bok choy. I'm dreaming, after all, but even dreams have occasional imperfections.

In reality I harbored more modest expectations. I had no real idea what, let alone how much, might grow into harvestable splendor as a result of my ministrations. I was determined to learn from my mistakes and hard experiences. That said, I knew even in the earliest days that I would be sorely disappointed if the field remained a barren lot. This is, after all, about food – about nourishment and the pleasures of consuming what one has helped to grow.

Nonetheless, I was a bit sobered by my quick deference to tangible results. If harvest is the only useful metric, then the potential for disillusionment and despair is vast and wide. But couldn't there be other, maybe even larger considerations touching soul and soil and self? And aren't some things larger even than the horizon of my awareness? If it is all merely about the perfunctory mechanics of "seed in," "edible out," then it doesn't really matter how it gets done. If productivity is the only viable measure, then pump it in and churn it out.

Even the writing of such possibilities, however, turns the words themselves as powdery and lifeless as the fields we have degraded by our vaunted "green revolution." Surely, as relevant and desirable as is a harvest, there must be something deeper and richer than merely filled baskets.

Wendell Berry, ever the observer of such things, writes by way of contrast that, "the real products of any year's work are the farmer's mind and the cropland itself." And then again more pointedly, "The finest growth that farmland can produce is a careful farmer." (from *Prayers and Sayings of the Mad Farmer*)

Building soil, growing a mind, and in so doing producing a careful farmer. I would, indeed, hope something edible matured from all these seeds, but if, instead, the best that I managed to accomplish was improving the soil and enlarging myself into something deeper and more careful, it would be a season of growing well and, in retrospect, appreciatively spent.

*Chores, chores, chores. Places to go, things to do. Then occasionally I wake from my drowse and for a few minutes every toad becomes a dragon, every lilac is a fiery fountain, and I am walking on pure light.* (Scott Russell Sanders, *Staying Put: Making a Home in a Restless World*, p. 137)

Winter progressed in its usual pendulous way, swinging between moderation and bitter cold. Eventually we filled the trays with potting soil and seeds and dispatched them to the greenhouse to proceed with their imperceptible work. The weather suddenly moderated and cleared to the extent that we could confront the tangled thicket between the house and the road. Driven in part by a desire to improve the appearance of the yard, and in part by a latent but resurfacing longing to fire up the power trimmer hibernating since autumn in the barn, we donned gloves, heavy clothes, and safety glasses. Without a shred of embarrassment, I retrieved the trimmer's owner's manual, reacquainted myself with the button and knob labels, perused the starting instructions, took a deep breath and pulled the rope. A few times. A cough. A gasoline-laced sputter. Ignition! Strapping on the shoulder strap and palming the handle bars (this isn't, after all, some puny twine spinner), I proceed into the sapling jungle like a gladiator into the coliseum, revving the engine every now and then as a kind of high combustion sneer.

The tripoint steel blade slashed and pruned and sawed and trimmed until, after what seemed like only minutes but proved to be more like an hour, the engine sputtered into silence; thirsty and out of gas. I paused to survey the carnage. To be sure, severed branches littered the area, waiting to be dragged out and piled. We had, indeed, made a credible start. What sobered me, however, was the slightness of the dent we had put in the task. Surveying the still-impregnable regions beneath the trees I tried to imagine the number of subsequent afternoons far more intensive than this one that would surely be required to accomplish prideful results. Chores, chores, chores strung together in infinite line. Peering into the thorny fortress, I half expected to see a gingerbread cottage and Hansel and Gretel's wicked witch interrupting her sweeping to crook her ugly finger beckoningly, menacingly in my direction.

And then a broken branch caught my eye. The diameter of my leg, the long branch had broken off high up the trunk and rested now, horizontally, on the tops of lesser bushes well out of reach and fortressed by the dense thicket surrounding; the victim of winter's winds and storms. Cradled there now, silent and stripped of its pride, it took on a kind of fascination. My first thought was a kind of scorn – "felled by a puny winter such as this one?" But scorn quickly gave way to wonder. This branch, I reflected, knows more of this place than I do. How long has it grown here? What has it observed; what has it shaded? What storms has it survived all these years, and what flaw – what weakness – caused it to succumb this particular year? At first glance it appeared a mighty and sturdy appendage, making its obvious vulnerability all the more surprising. But isn't it more a wonder that any branch actually survives, bent and laden and blown about as they become in winter?

I will yet need to hack my way in so that I can reach its lower extremities to pull and dislodge and, with any luck, extricate the woody corpse. But leaving it for now, I offer an appreciative benediction for the stately life it has both witnessed and embodied – high above it all.


Our first spring at Taproot Garden fooled us with an early beginning, not the kind of March we have learned the hard way to expect. Record setting warm temperatures jump-started trees into early bud break and me into an early apprehension that perhaps I had gotten seeds started too late. The average late freeze date for this site would not arrive for another five weeks, but all nature seemingly threw caution to the wind, forging ahead with its own kind of bull market. It would be awhile before we would know if the spring bubble would burst. Meanwhile, we dragged the grill out of mothballs, negotiated the early onset of allergy season, started enjoying long walks, and Tir and I the sunrise, the bird songs, and the donkey brays from the relaxing comfort of the deck extending off the eastern face of the house. It was precisely the location from which the three of us bid the previous day good night. The deck; in March; in Iowa. Who would have guessed?

There, in this early morning reverie, I mentally reviewed the to-do list and considered the swirling options. It wouldn't be possible for a person of my limited know-how to speed the seedlings along, but I could begin to lay the ground work for their garden debut. So, it had been that the prior day, with tape measure, twine, wooden stakes and mallet in hand, I took more accurate measure of the plot. Staking out the corners I discovered that my autumn eyeballing had abbreviated the northwest corner. The reel mower – purchased in a naïve fit of environmental friendliness – quickly demonstrated that it wasn't really designed for prairie grass. Nonetheless, it cleared well enough to suffice for the moment, though my pushing muscles remained angry for days.

Subsequent stakes and joining twine demarcated the garden's center aisle (obligatory for a minister's garden I thought) and the first levels of trenching. The fencing had arrived the day before, but I intended to stage that project after the trenches were dug. Then the guesswork began – or was it the crystal balling, voodoo, or rolling of the dice?

When to get started? I could surely begin preparing the planting spaces, but I didn't want the ground opened sooner than would be useful. I would need to prod delivery of the load of manure, but it would then need a place to go. Though I couldn't hurry the seedlings, fully two-thirds of the seeds I had ordered would go directly into the ground. As long as it stayed this warm and didn't revert to winter all should be fine. The seeds could certainly go in first, and be joined later by the seedlings when they were ready to transplant. Or I could wait until early May as originally planned.

My head was spinning with the possibilities. Thankfully, I didn't have to decide right away; besides, more rain was predicted for much of next week creating the opportunity to address all the unresolved preliminaries. What kind of tomato cages would be useful, how many, and where would I find them? It was past time to brush away the dried mud that still caked the tools from last year's experimental garden. I must get aggressive about shooing away the deer. When could we schedule the delivery of manure? And, of course, the digging. I had no idea how long that would take.

The cacophony of variables could have deafened and exhausted me, but the deck and the dog and the morning chorus stirred me like the anthem of a good choir. I sat comfortably, gliding in the deck chair; momentarily losing track of time. I would think it all through, eventually. "I am learning," I reminded myself – a humble disciple, not the Lord of the Harvest.

It would be some time before we had the chance to walk it. But in-between digging in the garden and nurturing the seedlings in the greenhouse, I blazed the trail completing the circle. Our predecessors on this property had mowed a wide path north from the back yard toward the tree line, forking eventually to the east and the simple fire circle long overgrown when we discovered it, and northwesterly toward the spring. Both legs, we quickly discovered, dead-ended in the trees, either by neglect or design. There's nothing wrong with turning around and retracing steps you have just imprinted in the grass, but our psyches or souls prefer more orbital patterns. We envisioned extending the northwesterly lane into an arcing reach that would eventually, and without regression, lead a nature-minded stroller back to the starting point.

Seven months into our landed living, the dead-end remained. I would get to it, I kept promising the two of us, deterred by no particular impediment save my own seemingly pathological resistance to leaving a mark of my own – on the land, to be sure, but sometimes I think on life itself. I dream well, but as happened that first time I climbed the ladder to the swimming pool's high diving board decades before, more often than not I peer off the end into the distant and watery abyss, hesitate, and climb with a clinging shiver back down. You would think I'd be over that at this age – especially over an act as simple and impermanent as mowing a scenic path through a grassy field. For whatever reason, and perhaps simply for reasons of greater importance, other projects had pushed ahead of this one in the queue – trimming, sawing, chipping, seeding, trenching, tree-planting, bulb-planting, successively mowing. Besides, before the path could be cut there would need to be a plan – exactly where to bend it, between which trees to thread it, how artfully to shape it – and then a survey to clear any blade-bending rocks.

I can't account for the timing. Indeed, there wasn't really time. This single day was crammed between two trips, and rain was predicted. Laundry piles needed washing before repacking. Fresh milk to buy for Lori at the closest market, and a book to claim at the library. The car needed gas, the seedlings in the greenhouse needed tending, and the sentimental "Thousand Blossoms" aster plant received in the mail as a gift from the daughter of a beloved friend needed planting – all in addition to mowing before curtain time at the theater in the evening.

It just sort of happened. Mowing along in the coolness of the morning, I reached the northern dead-end, and before I knew it, a lusty glance to the west had escaped and the tractor followed after. I had no scouted design or cautionary survey, only the throb of the diesel engine, the whirling of the blades first high then low, uncharted grassland and my face stretched into an adventurous and satisfied smile.

Days would elapse before I had a chance to walk our new path, but as we boarded a plane at the Des Moines airport that afternoon, I knew the mark on our land had finally been made; the trail blazed; the circle completed.

And for reasons only the soul understands, the smile remains.


MIDWAY THROUGH THAT FIRST GARDEN SEASON I experienced two catches in my throat, albeit from oppositely toned stimuli. Watering the garden and then surrendering myself to the garden trenches and their riotous weeds, I seized my first opportunity to converse with the toddler vegetables on a first-name basis. Obscured by the tufting grass blades in one area, it happily turns out, lettuce was actually appearing. No signs yet of peppers on the greenhouse transplants, but the plants seemed to be thriving. The potatoes – all three varieties – appeared positively festive; the purple cabbage, sage, collard greens and squashes were meanwhile flexing their own burgeoning muscles.

It was, however, the tomatoes that made me giggle. They were blooming. Lots of blossoms on lots of plants. I'm not clear

ßß

why the tomatoes had risen to "favorite child" status. In my head, I was every bit as anxious for the myriad pepper plants to go into labor and eager for the squashes and beets and all the others. But for whatever reason the tomatoes captured my soul. Maybe it was the extra attention they demanded in the sprouting – first watering and watching, then moving up to more spacious abodes in the large plastic beverage cups, and then finally being the last to dip their roots in the garden proper. Perhaps it was the fully developed vision of their derivative uses via the canning kitchen we were waiting to employ. Perhaps it was because the varieties I selected have particular whimsical appeal. Or maybe it was, like Guy Clark's song says,

*"There's only two things that money can't buy*
*and that's true love and homegrown tomatoes."*

I don't know. Suffice it to say the appearance of those small yellow blossoms was like the first twinkling light of Advent, with the next several weeks – OK, the next *several* weeks – feeling like a child's anticipation of Christmas.

I can't say that it completely took the song out of my step when I steered my way along the bean aisle, but the tune certainly shifted to a minor key. There I could see that something had been getting better acquainted than I with my cannellini and calypso beans. Upon closer inspection I could see that neither the favas nor Good Mother Stallards had been immune. Having sprouted vigorously, indeed almost playfully, with a delightfully leafy canopy, the row was now perilously near nakedness, more spindly stems than covering leaves.

Something had been grazing, but whether rodent, insect or fowl, I couldn't yet say. The fence, designed to withstand rabbits and raccoons and even deer, allowed birds to land and dance within the compound. But the damage didn't strike me as beak induced. If I were a betting man, I would say it looked like rabbit nibbling, but up until then I hadn't seen any such thing anywhere near the fencing. In front of the house, yes; beside the barn, you bet. But I hadn't seen them sniffing curiously around the garden aching for a tunnel in, though I supposed they could be coming at night. Bugs of some kind could be the culprit – a worm or some such predator – but you would think you might see one hanging around. So far, nothing.

Nothing, that is, except this oddly melancholic intersection of the bean row horror and the tomato blossoms' hope. I grieved for my beans, but whatever it was had better stay away from the tomatoes, I declared. I might just have to set up a chair in the garden and spend the night on patrol –

with a stick,

or a gun,

or a prayer.

I'm not much of an aim with either a stick or a gun, but I was willing to believe that God's heart, too, has a soft spot for home-grown tomatoes.


I READ NOW OF "HELICOPTER PARENTS" – the 21st-century pattern of dubious child-rearing best characterized by the teenager who complains that "mother hovers over me like a helicopter." Teachers and school administrators are too-well acquainted with these types;

classrooms, principals' offices and dorm rooms having become veritable helipads for the landing of overly zealous parents who have taken "child advocacy" to steroidal levels.

Suddenly, however, I understood.

It had been our intention, ever since moving to Taproot Garden, to "put up" the excess of the harvest. When moving in and arranging the household, we established a canning kitchen in the lower level, equipped with shelving, counter-tops, a utility sink and a stove. Along the way we accumulated books on the subject, attended seminars, and eventually purchased supplies. All we lacked was the harvest. That, however, we were confident was only a matter of time.

But then we panicked. We had never canned before; and we were going to learn on our own precious harvest? The tomatoes and peppers and cucumbers and the rest that we had labored over, weeded around, sprinkled around and sung to since they were seed cells in the greenhouse? What if (as was completely likely) we screwed it up? "Absolutely not!" we declared. All we needed was some practice.

We had ordered jars online, though they hadn't yet been delivered. Target, however, had them on sale in the local store, so we stocked up. Shortly before closing time one late-summer Saturday we hurried through the Downtown Farmer's Market and snatched up discounted boxes of "ugly" tomatoes, Serrano peppers and garlic. Heading home we detoured by Costco to procure large containers of organic strawberries plus the essential water bath pot for the canning, and headed home.

Looking back, the rest of the weekend dissolved into something of a blur of sanitizing, boiling, chopping, mashing, simmering, filling, lowering, raising, rereading instructions, and listening in the end for that almost musical telltale "pop" that signals the lid has miraculously sealed the jar. And sampling with a satisfied smile from the small dishes we had set aside.

The result?

•*18 pints of strawberry preserves (half spiced, half traditional)*

•*18 pints of tomato sauce*

•*8 pints of salsa*

This, from the practice session! Meanwhile, looking ahead, we still had the produce ripening in our own garden. Assuming, that is, we could actually bear the thought of picking it, chopping it, and submerging its jars beneath the roiling boil of the canner.

Because I now recognized that we had become –

"helicopter gardeners."


THE CONCEPT OF "RIPENESS" HAS, I SUPPOSE, always felt a little murky. I recall asking a farmer friend to explain it to me one afternoon when we were at his farm picking up our share. His first response – derived from his more technical side – had something to do with the fruit reaching its complete capacity to reproduce the plant. I had something more basic in mind – like how you know when to pick something? He subsequently offered up a kind of horticultural behaviorist account that still, today, seems more mystically poetic than helpful – about how the plant rather offers up the fruit by getting out of the way, as opposed to its protective hiding during the maturation process. Perhaps to the trained observer that all makes some sense, but not to this clumsy, ham-handed novice. I still navigate between the overly zealous (which generally provides me with more than my share of "green") and the overly cautious (which almost disdainfully mushes into my palm, as if to say, "What kept you so long?").

To my natural ambiguity I have now added a new stimulus for harvest hand-wringing: it's dangerous out there! Never mind the chicken wire and the mesh, rabbits can breach my defenses at any moment, hopping over or burrowing under. And no self-respecting deer would actually be intimidated by my fortifications. From the very beginning the fencing I had erected was designed to deter, not prevent. And then, of course, bugs and beetles and fungi and aphids all need my garden to accomplish their life-cycle and therefore, any of them could invade and infest and destroy overnight. My precious harvest is vulnerable out there, like a child walking alone through the park after dark. Who can calculate all the evils that could befall?

Thus the paradox. Having things growing in the garden delights us with its potential while at the same time burdens us with its needs and our responsibilities. Actually have things growing in the garden is a gift, but also an immense responsibility. I certainly don't want to leave produce out in the garden to rot, but I do want it to enjoy the full resplendency of its ripeness. Then again, I don't want to leave it vulnerable any longer than is absolutely necessary. But...

Perhaps my indecision is a little like that parenting image to which I earlier alluded – judging when to shelter and when to let go. Or like poker – knowing "when to hold 'em and when to fold 'em."

You get the point. This is worrisome business. It's a wonder that any of it – including the gardener – survives.


The heat, that first summer, started breaking records – both the temperatures and their duration. Drought conditions only exacerbated the problem. After a stingy winter that gave up remarkably little snow to replenish the soil, spring and summer had thus far opted to repent of last years' flooding by withholding moisture altogether. Farmers across the Midwest wrung their hands, watching their crops dry up. Meanwhile, I felt personally chastised one day in late July when the water authority for the area looked down their noses at us gluttonous citizens and the copious gallons of water we were using every day. Voluntary water rationing was put in force.

"Sure," I complained to myself, "but I have collard greens I am trying to mature – to say nothing of all those tomatoes still ripening. And did I mention the seeds I planted last week gasping for life in all this dry heat? Rationing doesn't seem like much of an option right now. I know, I know; that's selfish and short-sighted, but…"

In the meantime, I noticed something of a miracle. Back in May, I had planted three kinds of okra seeds, and though the plants had sprouted and flourished, they had flourished low – small, that is. What should be a bush of 24-36 inches by that number of growing days had stalled at around six inches. They looked healthy. They just looked small. And then I began to see blossoms.

I had to admit that I had never noticed okra blossoms before – squash blossoms, yes, but not okra. But there they were. And then, suddenly, okra – two different kinds: several "Hill Country Reds" and several of the traditional green "Clemson Spineless." As welcome as they were – as gratefully giddy as I was – I had to admit that they looked a little foolish; like Shaquille O'Neal riding a tricycle. Phallic fruitings not modestly veiled by the leaves – there weren't enough leaves to offer much virtue – but this time protruding vertically right out the top.

I wasn't complaining. I would happily take them – albeit with a smile.

AND THEN IT SEEMED LIKE ANCIENT HISTORY – or only yesterday, depending on the angle of vision. Our first year of residence at Taproot Garden was coming to a close. Eleven months earlier we had moved to this property with a household's worth of packed boxes and a vision, with excitement and more than a little apprehension over the implications of what we had done. Less than a year – not so long when measured by the calendar, but an eon, all else considered. In the intervening months we had trimmed trees, cleared brush, planted trees, built a greenhouse, commissioned and planted a sign, designed a garden, ordered and planted seeds, cleared the target area, dug trenches, staked and strung a fence, and planted. Planting gave way to watering, weeding; weeding and watering; contending with rabbits, adding more fence, weeding and watering, watering and weeding, contending with deer, waiting and watching, watering and weeding. And weeding and watering.

There develops, in the practice of it all, an almost drone-like character to the tending – a rhythmic, centering monotony only occasionally interrupted by a brief rain or a schedule conflict. Watering, weeding, observing the growthful progress. We felt a certain giddiness watching the progression from stem to leaf to flower to bud and finally that blush of color. But still the drone – the weeding, the watering, the studious observation and the waiting.

We experienced a delicious euphoria at the first tomato plucked and the companion pepper snipped. But it doesn't pay to overly indulge in self-congratulation. A garden, I have learned, is like a river – always moving, always in motion; or maybe a glacier, given the almost imperceptible pace, but moving nonetheless.

And the drone, I have discovered, is hypnotic. Barely shaking off sleep, I get out early to preempt the heat, yank the standpipe's handle, will my palm into compliance with the shape of the hose, and set about the routine. The drone buoys me along the paces, watering and then weeding, noticing.

Suddenly I realize I am missing something important: the harvest. After those initial offerings, I have slipped back into my routine, forgetting that growing things inexorably move toward ripeness – the payoff of all the effort.

So, each day I learned to will into active consciousness the instruction to actually harvest something that could be growing underground, but could just as easily be maturing unnoticed before my eyes; to allow myself a momentary arrival in the midst of this ongoing journey; the crunch of a fresh raw okra, the juice of a ripe tomato dripping off my chin, the spicy bite of a pepper just off the stem.

And in so pausing, I stepped out of the lulling drone and paid a different, more flavorful attention.


THE TRUTH IS THAT I HAD PRACTICALLY FORGOTTEN ABOUT THEM. Charge me with negligence if you must, but they hadn't given me much cause for titillated anticipation. I had sown the seeds in mid-May, and the several times I had "dipsticked" their progress through the summer they had demonstrated almost supernatural antipathy toward growth. More than once I had mistaken their willowy little fronds for weeds, and no doubt more than one was aborted through just such confusion. As late as August, when a young visitor accidentally uprooted one, it could have been mistaken for a jaundiced pea.

All this, plus the fact that I didn't have much invested in them besides space. I hadn't actually intended to plant carrots in the first place. The seeds were a free gift from the seed company from which I had ordered several other varietals of higher interest for this inaugural season. A bonus. An afterthought. I had committed them to the ground, and largely left them alone.

So it was that in the middling days of November, in the course of my ongoing winterization of the garden – dismantling fence panels, uprooting steel posts, mulching, manuring and the like – that I happened a glance in their direction. Ready, I must admit, to have the spaces officially put to bed, I determined to dig up whatever might remain – if anything. There were, I could see upon closer inspec-

tion, glimpses of orange peeking up above the surface; more, I soon discovered, down below. Dozens of them – short and stumpy little Parisienne Carrots. A harvest where I least expected it.

More insight springs from this windfall than I really want to internalize – my biggest harvest from my most neglected and forgotten sowing – but I resolved to stew on that another time. For the present, I continued my approach to winter yet again humbled and grateful for this serendipitous gift of the garden – a penultimate harvest, as it turns out, since I did eventually leave the immature kale still valiantly growing, for a final harvest another day.

Looking back, that first harvest was a wild success. We stocked the freezer. The canning kitchen got a busy workout, turning out red salsa and green salsa, pickled beets and okra and cucumbers. We even experimented with fermentation, shredding cabbage that miraculously became sauerkraut. The individual specimens may not have been that pretty or impressive, but we weren't gardening for photographs. We were here to grow food.

But did we actually learn anything, or were we simply the beneficiaries of nature's gracious largesse?

# CHAPTER NINE

# WITH THE HELP OF ALPACAS

*The gardener answered, "I'll dig around it
and put some manure on it to make it grow."*

Luke 13:8 (CEV)

T ir's ears never relaxed.

The late September autumn evenings, those first few weeks in residence at our new home, were lovely. Calling a halt to the day's unpacking, we would settle out on the deck with our beloved Welsh Corgi who, like the two of us, was familiar only with the sights and sounds of the city. These evenings were animated by very different stimulations. Squirrels were nothing new, but these numbers certainly were. Birds had darted in and out of the townhouse development back in the city but hardly this diversity of them. There were, in other words, continuities – in kind, if not quantity. And then there were the new introductions. It would not be unusual, we soon discovered, to notice an opossum exploring the yard in this rural setting, or curious deer nuzzling the tree line. Raccoons were no stranger, nor the occasional garden snake or wildcat or wild turkey.

And then there were the sounds! Sitting out on the deck, perched safely in a lap, Tir was transfixed, his body tense with high alert. His head tilted from side to side as one strange sound stole his attention from another; ears, peaked, rotated slightly for a clarifying angle.

It was, we soon discovered, an interesting neighborhood into which we had moved. Our attentions, in those first months of our residency here had been almost militarily focused on settling in, extracting all contents from their boxes, flattening those boxes for the recycling bin, sorting the wrapping paper into what we could use later and what would need to be recycled, finding both a logical, convenient, and/or artful place for all our worldly possessions. In other words, creating order out of chaos, the task of the first day of creation, as I recall from my Genesis 1 study.

Our world had been confined to the crowded rooms and the view immediately outside our windows. But weary with the work of the day, sometimes with a plate of food and other times with simply a body of tired muscles and a puppy, we would collapse into a chair outside. Even there work beckoned us, albeit of a radically different sort. Evening deck time was part relaxation, part "name that sound" game. It was easy to identify the donkeys off somewhere in the distance, and we could speculate about the source of the various snorts and harrumphs. But what was that horrifying cry – something of a screech, and clearly country fauna, but with an eerily human quality that almost sounded like a child screaming for help? Tir remained vigilant, certain that defensive action – or a rescue mission – was imminent.

Soon we learned that the anguished sound was simply the vocal styling of the peacock flock from the exotic animal farm down the road – an expansive property cohabited by miniature goats, miniature donkeys, four camels, a herd of watusi, and at least one well-hidden zebra only rarely seen, among other less-identifiable species. We eventually learned that it had all started with a single camel that the man of the house deemed necessary for the parades his Shriner group occasionally walked in. One camel led to more and, as the couple attended more and more exotic animal sales, husband and wife each discovered new fascinations and acquisitional appetites. Over the years it had spiraled out of control. I know how that sort of thing can happen.

While all that exotic splendor resides across the way and at the end of the road, which was increasingly the destination of morning walks and explorations, even more fascinations occupied the sheds closer to home. Art and Kathy had retired some years before and settled on the acreage adjacent to ours. Excepting the exotic animal habitat which occupied almost 200 acres, the general shape and size of these several tracts alongside of ours were virtually identical ten-acre rectangles extending away from the road. Beyond that general similarity, however, the properties are wildly different. Each is unique in terrain, topography and character. Some are flat; one slopes inwardly toward a dividing ravine; several have ponds fed by a spring deep in the woods.

Our neighbors had cleared some trees, developed the pond, and built a house along with two sheds that housed alpacas. Twenty-five or so of them at any given time. Gray, brown, white, and black. Some petite, some large for their bread. Some on the wise and mature side; generally a few babies and juveniles. With their long and agile legs and gangly necks, they roam inside their fence, grazing and lazing and noting the arrival of strangers. Eventually they noted us, along with Tir, whom they observed passing by with increasing regularity on the road out front. As our comfort level grew, our passes got closer and closer to the fence and, as our acquaintance with Art and Kathy deepened, we got comfortable feeding and petting the gentle animals.

Gentle, and it's difficult not to use the word, "sweet." Alpacas are kindly animals that only rarely get cross with each other over some presumed offense or advantage. More typically they explore, graze, relax, and monitor their surroundings like silent sentinels. Sometimes described as "llamas that don't spit," they are, indeed, companionable and amenable to the visitations of strangers. And new neighbors with a dog.

We had first learned of alpacas while visiting Ecuador some years before, where the garments and textiles made of alpaca wool are famously and finely made, prized by locals and sought after by tourists. It was, then, their coats that drew my attention as we became better acquainted – the diverse colors and the feel of the fiber. True to purpose, these wooly neighbors are shorn one time each year, in the spring, and the resulting bags of shavings are sold for weaving. It occurred to me, however, that the alpacas might have an earthier and more constant value. They wander, yes, and eat and grow wool. They also poop, and poop I could use.

I researched the subject and learned that much can be said about the value of using alpaca manure as a garden soil amendment. I'll spare you the details and simply note that it works – a beneficial soil conditioner that helps retain moisture, adds organic matter along with necessary nutrients like nitrogen and potassium and phosphorus, and, for various reasons like an absence of weed seeds, can be preferable to the more common manure of cows and horses. All of which sounded good to me. Cows and horses I didn't have. Alpacas, on the other hand, lived right next door – along with Art, who must daily muck out the sheds and do *something* with the bucketed collection. What, I wondered aloud to Art one day, if that *something* became a pile near our garden? I'm guessing he still shakes his head in baffled amusement every time he lugs a few buckets through the trees and empties them onto that resulting pile. Not everybody, I recognize, lives in hot pursuit of a manure pile in his yard, but I am thrilled that he humors me, and am grateful for the alpaca's regular generosity.

Every fall, once we have completed the harvest, I press the wheel barrow into service, hauling loads of the manure inside the garden gate where I dump and spread the contents on the rows. What looks like a mountainous accumulation very quickly becomes a level plain. It takes a lot of manure to cover the long beds with an inch or so each year, but the alpacas are clearly up to the challenge. I typically run out of energy and initiative before I run out of manure. Which isn't a problem. There is always next season.

# Chapter Ten

# With the Chickens as Teachers

*If I hadn't started painting,
I would have raised chickens.*

Grandma Moses

Before a box was even packed, as soon as word began to spread that we were "moving to a farm," everyone – especially those with little experience of such things – offered ready suggestions. "You have to get a pickup," we heard a thousand times.

"No," I routinely replied, "I have no interest in – or use for – a pickup."

"You have to get chickens," was the inevitable sequel.

"You have to be kidding," I suggested. "We are moving out there to grow vegetables. You know, dig in the soil and sprout things. I have no interest in any part of keeping chickens – the hassle, the smell, the 'chickenness' of it. There will be no chickens. I repeat, No chickens!"

Of course, now we use the pickup we shortly thereafter acquired to pick up feed for… the chickens. Even now, I have no real clarity as to how it came to pass. One minute we were resolved to never have even a single chicken, and the next we were creating a home for many. It must be the country air and the absence of chemicals on the vegetables. Or, more likely, the constant pictures of and stories about the various breeds in the constant trickle of farm related magazines that began finding their way into our mailbox.

Three years into our farming adventure, the idea took hold. Perhaps we were gaining confidence or had comfortably plateaued. We had softened to the idea of expanding our experience here and chickens began to sound… well… interesting. If I had once thought chickens were simply "chickens" – a monolithic category of otherwise indistinguishable poultry – I quickly learned otherwise. The variety is almost endless. The sizes, the colors, the temperaments, the eggs. I was well-acquainted with white-shelled eggs and had heard rumors of brown, but I had no idea that eggs came in many colors.

There were meat birds and layers and "dual purpose" breeds; there were cold-hardy chickens and heat-tolerant varieties, heritage breeds and production hybrids. There were exotics, and there were commoners. One could purchase them as baby chicks or as "started pullets" – the poultry equivalents of teenagers. They are available by mail or at the local farm supply store. I simply had no idea.

As we inched our way closer to the edge of the diving board, we determined that raising baby chicks sounded like a lot of work – specialized feed, monitoring and managing temperatures 24-hours a day in some protected environment lest they get the sniffles and die. We were curious, but not *that* curious. For one thing, we like our sleep; for another, we didn't need all that pressure. It's one thing to neglect a seedling in the garden, but something else entirely to bury a baby chick. We found a large and reputable source for adolescent birds in a small community a couple of hours north of us, selected two of the breeds online, chose a delivery week near what we hoped would be the end of winter, and proceeded to click "place your order." When I balked at the cost of shipping I called and volunteered to drive and pick up the birds myself.

"We only have the day-old chicks here. The older birds come from Texas."

You have to be kidding me. Texas? We were getting Lone Star layers? Suddenly it all felt "right" as I began to anticipate their "cluck" with a twang to match my own.

Lori, ever more practical than her husband, interrupted my fantasy of an Alamo-themed coop with the reminder that, as of yet, we had no coop at all – or a thought-out plan for where to put it. Details!

It turns out that *where* to locate a coop on our property was a question more easily resolved than *what* to locate. If there is a dizzying variety of chickens from which to choose, the options for how to house them are exponentially greater. There are crude ones, elegant ones, artistic ones and makeshift ones. There are stationary ones, mobile ones, wooden ones, metal ones, plastic ones. There are coops converted from shipping containers, dog houses, tool sheds and derelict buses. There are coops with electric lights and solar powered automatic doors; there are heated ones, plumbed ones, multi-roomed ones and wifi-connected ones; Amish-built ones and injection molded ones. Every variation, of course, purports to be the perfect living environment, apart from which chickens are left at the mercy of predators, the elements, and the vicissitudes of a deprived and diminished life. In selecting one there are cleaning issues to consider, laying and gathering logistics to incorporate, ventilation to ensure but drafts to prevent. Are feeders built in or must they be added? And what about water? Is it sturdy enough to keep out varmints? And... et cetera.

One constant, however, stuck out among the options. All of them were expensive. Wondering if this was such a good idea after all, we nonetheless pressed ahead. We came across a builder in southern Missouri whose coops looked appealing. Sturdy and well-built, they offered the features that seemed essential to us, along with options we decided might be useful. We took a deep breath, wrote the big check, and scheduled a satisfactory date for delivery prior to the anticipated arrival of the hens. And then wondered all over again what we had gotten ourselves into.

Other problematic details emerged. We liked the idea of "free-range," but were simultaneously worried about safety. This is, after all, "nature." We delight in watching deer routinely drift through our property, but are less excited about the opossums and the raccoons and the coyotes. We've seen more than one wildcat on the edge of the woods, and while the hawks are stately in their flight and the foxes graceful as they leap their way through the grasses, all of them would love a chicken dinner every now and then. A fence of some kind seemed in order – preferably electrified – and gun turrets for the guards.

I'm only kidding about the guards.

Sort of.

Since the coop we purchased had wheels that would allow us to relocate it from time to time, some kind of a movable fence seemed a logical accessory. An Iowa company advertised a simple, easily moved net fence to which an energizer could be connected. We calculated the needed length, added on a portable solar package, and set to work readying ourselves for the hobby enterprise we never thought we wanted.

ßß

AND THEN WE WENT CONDO.

At least the chickens did.

Because it isn't all bucolic bliss.

It all started with a funeral. One of the first group of eight chickens that set up housekeeping in our coop died a few days after arriving. I have no medical explanation, but since the birds came from Waco, Texas, we concluded that she didn't much care for the change in climate. Iowa winters aren't for everybody, after all, and this particular winter was challenging even by Iowa standards. Never mind that the ladies arrived in the waning weeks of the arctic grip; the change would have been startling nonetheless.

From eight, then down to seven. The loss was especially grievous because while all four of the breeds represented were handsome in their own way, this one – a Silver-laced Wyandotte, with its vivid blotches of black and white – was beautiful. True, one of the pair remained, but we opted to adopt a replacement. OK, we opted to replace the lost *one* with *two*.

ßß

But they weren't going to be available for another six weeks. My replacement juices actively flowing, and there being so many appealing breeds, it only made sense (in some parallel universe) to order additionally a pair of one of those other options - Buff Orpington - that would be available in a couple of weeks.

And so there we were: *four* hens to replace the *one* we lost. This is the kind of math I understand.

The impending arrivals created, however, a new problem. Chickens, as it turns out, do not automatically get along. Like new neighbors who must first get accustomed to one other across the backyard fence before extending an invitation to dinner, chickens must be segregated for the first couple of weeks – within view of each other, mind you – before adjusting their established pecking order in non-lethal ways. This was one of my early educations in the chicken yard. Since childhood I had heard the phrase, "pecking order," but had no idea that the concept actually derived from observable behavior among flocks of chickens.

It does, and they do.

This evolutionary behavior created a problem. A group of randomly chosen chickens is not a neighborhood, and no dividing fence protected those at the bottom of the pecking order. How were we to segregate chickens in a single coop? The answer, of course, was the acquisition of a secondary coop and run, which I didn't really want to afford but to which I saw little alternative. I considered various homemade options, but even though the birds would only be housed there temporarily, I hesitated. After all, we are talking about me, and tools. Usually not a promising combination.

To allay the concerns of friends and family members who had already started looking up the number of the Society for the Prevention of Cruelty to Animals, Craig's List connected me with an industrious soul in the heart of Des Moines who made chicken

coops close enough to my price range that the problem could be agreeably solved.

And so it came to pass that our first poultry problem was easily solved. But, what of the rest?

SOMETIMES CRISES ARE IMPOSED UPON US. Other times we create our own.

In the following instance, I will assert the compensatory defense that we had been busy. Aware that bad weather was predicted, I had attacked the overgrown grass in the dog run, trimmed a little more in the garden, pulled some extra weeds, restocked the chickens' feed and water, and then got busy noting all said accomplishments in my journal. By the time Lori got home, the sun was setting and dinner yet to prepare. Shortly thereafter, sated and weary, we stacked dishes in the kitchen sink, took the dog out one more time and shuffled off to bed. It wasn't until the storm was erupting in all its violent splendor that I realized I hadn't cooped the chickens. And admitted with comfortable shame that I wasn't willing to crawl out of bed, dress and venture out into the tornado-warning and rain-drenching out of doors, braving the thunder and lightening and high winds to see if the chickens were secure.

The main coop, I was confident, would be OK. It has a long and low profile with a curved silhouette. Its doors were open and so I worried over possible predators, but I hoped the electric fence would provide some insurance; hoped as well that the storm would incentivize their behavior as much as it did mine. And hoped that most of the rain would be kept out.

It was the annex that concerned me – that inexpensive, secondary coop temporarily housing the newer arrivals. Because I had placed that coop only a short distance from the fence-line, I feared some predator would smell helpless prey and dig its way in. At a more basic level I was concerned that the high winds could even topple it. It wasn't, after all, the finest piece of architecture. Beyond that, the chicken door opens on the north face, straight into the wind and the rain. An elevated roost would offer some remove from a soupy floor – the nesting boxes above even more. But I fretted about fright and soggy feathers and cursed my inattention.

When the dogs, a number now grown to two with the addition of another Welsh Corgi named "Nia," nudged me awake at their usual pre-light hour, I took them out and then stood sentry in the sunroom, bracing myself for whatever first light might reveal. As black gave way to gray, I could make out the outline of the fence and see that it was still intact. Nothing had breached the perimeter. And then movement out of the corner of my eye. Unconfined, the hens were already out bantering around the chicken yard, busily searching for surfacing worms. I dared to count. Everything tallied. All seemed well, and like teenagers whose parents are out of town, the girls strutted their emancipation. They were coming and going as they pleased. As is common when I'm watching them, I laughed. And sighed with relief.

Later, breakfasted and dressed, I surveyed the condition of the coops. As I had anticipated, the main coop was fine. The run was understandably soggy, but the sleeping quarters were high and dry. My surprise came with the annex. Not only was it upright, exactly as I had left it. It was, like its fancier neighbor, dry and comfortable. The feed dispenser and waterer were both empty, as though the occupants had partied through the storm, but other than that all was perfectly in order. Given my twilight worrying, I almost begrudged them their serenity. Almost. I refilled their provisions and penitentially layered in more pine shavings to bolster their bedding.

More storms were in the forecast. I was happy for any additional rain; but despite the previous night's happy ending, I resolved to be more diligent in the nights to come. Eventually I would learn the hard way how deadly such forgetful negligence can be. This time, however, I dodged the consequences and at least temporarily learned a lesson. Next time, the coop doors will be closed and latched, with the chickens safely bedded and battened down inside. And with any luck I, too, will sleep in peace.

CHICKENS DIFFER. That shouldn't have come as a surprise to me, but it was a revelation. If we had considered it, our education into such genetic variables was well underway. Nia, our newly acquired female tri-colored Welsh Corgi, could not be more different from Tir, our male champagne colored "older brother." While Tir is constantly underfoot, Nia prefers to keep her distance. Tir enjoys cuddling. Nia growls at any intimacy not her idea. These two, moreover, are startlingly different from our first Corgi we had come to love many years earlier. Dogs are unique. Each of the alpacas next door is distinct. It should have been obvious that chickens would be as well.

ßß

It should have been, but apparently I had not been paying attention. The differences are not confined to their feathers. The eggs are different as well. Brown ones of myriad hue and, now, blue and green ones.

Which usually precipitates further questions, and amazement. The questions - like "Who knew there was such a thing as a blue egg?" - don't surprise me. Eggs, after all, in our overly industrialized food system are almost universally white. Diversity comes in size - small, medium, large and extra-large - but rarely in color. Only recently could brown eggs be routinely found in a grocery store refrigerator case, but even then relegated to the edges as something of a quaint novelty. Blue or green eggs aren't likely to gain any shelf space any time soon. Little wonder that few people know such things exist.

THE AMAZEMENT, HOWEVER, IS MORE DIFFICULT TO EXPLAIN — amazement that multiple breeds exist, and amazement that we would choose more than one of them. Of the eleven birds developing into a flock who called Taproot Garden home, two were Ameraucana, two were Black Australorp, two were Buff Orpington, two were Red Star, two were Barred Rock, and one was a Wyandotte. Beautiful, I would say - every one of them - and beautifully diverse. These six hardly exhaust the options. Hatchery catalogs are as thick and colorfully evocative as seed catalogs - glossy photographs of all manner of sizes and colors and purposes and temperaments. Heritage breeds, as I mentioned before, hybrids and cross-breeds; but then there is the entire United Nations of options: Asian breeds, European breeds, African breeds, American breeds. As the seasons progressed we would add the likes of Speckled Sussex, Mottled Java, Buff Brahma, Marraduna Basque, Bielefelder, Blue Copper Maran, Crested Cream Legbar, Lavender Orpington, Mint Cream Bar - among others. And still that only scratches the surface of possibilities. The diversity is almost endless.

Sort of like people. And vegetables. And, I'm guessing, everything else around us. I remember my own surprise at discovering multiple varieties of broccoli. And tomatoes. And lettuce. Creation is an orchestra, not just in its aggregate, but within each instrumental part. There aren't just "flutes," but bass flutes and alto flutes, tenor and soprano flutes. Neither are there simply "drums." And we aren't just people; we are all kinds of people - "red and yellow, black and white" as the old children's song observes, but also short and tall and quiet and loud and any number of other diversities we are still getting our minds around.

I began watching our chickens, our veritable symphony of them - each breed with physical characteristics and personality traits, but also each bird with its own unique traits.

And laughing.

And marveling at them all.

Diverse individuals living as a community within the same backyard coop - pushing and shoving and pecking each other from time to time and haggling over a remnant scrap of food, not unlike the people who tend them; but also nestling close together on the roost at night for companionship and warmth.

A cacophony of diversity, for the most part getting along.

Do you suppose we humans could try to learn a lesson from the chickens? Try to live with, yes, diversity and pecking orders, but also with an understanding that I won't try to make your life miserable unless you try to grab what is mine. It would never be perfect, but we could be better. We could thrive.

HOME. Some describe it in relational terms – "where, when you go there, they have to take you in," according to Robert Frost. For Dorothy, lost in the land of Oz, there was "no place like home," and there would be no relief until she could physically return there. Emily Dickinson took the opposite view – that "where thou art, that is home." But for at least two of the chickens, Pliny the Elder got it right: "home is where the heart is." And their heart is very specifically located.

It had started a few weeks earlier when the two Red Stars arrived. Following conventional wisdom, I settled them into the coop annex – that modest secondary structure located in the general vicinity of the primary coop but separated by mesh fencing to protect the new arrivals from pecking order battles that can mount into deadly escalations. As I mentioned, the idea is for the settled hens to become familiar with the new neighbors long enough to forget that they haven't always been together.

The requisite two weeks passed, and I introduced the Stars to the larger flock. Afternoon passed without incident, but that evening as everyone was drifting inside the run, Lori noticed that one of the Barred Rocks was roughing up the smaller of the two Stars. She heroically intervened and reestablished the previous segregation. In subsequent days I united the flock during daylight hours but returned the Red Stars to their annex for roosting.

Weeks progressed with this arrangement intact. Days were spent in united free-ranging, but as darkness approached the division reemerged – the older hens ascending the ramp into their coop, while the newer two drifted over to the edge of the fence line near the annex, waiting for me to help them home. Safety was no longer the issue – they were all perfectly happy in each other's company. Rainstorms had sent them all running amiably for common shelter. They share the same food and water and nesting boxes. They scurry around happily side by side most of the day.

Then it was as though dusk blows some kind of a whistle. Regardless of the day's events, nightfall sent the older hens up and the newer hens over – quite literally over the fence – with help. The two would follow me over to the edge and squat, waiting for me to pick them up, one by one, and drop them into their own little corner of their own little world.

I'll admit that it was sweet. I will also acknowledge that it became tiresome. We would be sitting on the deck, enjoying the free entertainment of the girls pecking their way around the enclosure when, as if on a signal, the two groups moved in their separate directions. The Stars kindly but assertively would look our way, as if to say, "We'd like to go to bed now." And I would comply.

It could be, I suppose, the residue of traumatic memories - a kind of Freudian imposition of unspoken boundaries. But I don't think so. By all appearances they were content in each other's company. And then there are those who locate responsibility squarely at my feet. I had been complicit, they argue, in patterning a habit the hens were now unwilling to break. To some extent, I'll concede their point. I am an indulgent flockster. Our neighbor, often observing these tender routines, laughed and said, "I hope, when I die, I'll come back as one of your chickens." Fair enough. I'm an enabler.

But I am convinced there was more to it than mere routine. More than memory. More than habit. I rather believe, as Pliny surmised, it has something to do with the location of their heart. It's as though they were saying, "We'll spend our days in whatever way makes sense – in wild adventure or in pursuit of basic sustenance, in deep contemplation or lively social engagement – but at the end of the day we'd prefer to simply go home. Where our comb-headed, feathery little heart is."

Which, come to think of it, sounds a lot like me.

So, I suppose I am good with it. But it sure would be nice if I could teach them to close their eyes, click their heels together and cluck something like, "There's no place like the annex…" and miraculously be there without my assistance.

But I doubt the ruby slippers would fit their little claws.


The process of segregation and integration never gets easier. New birds arrive, they spend their time apart, and eventually the day arrives for the "great migration." I'll say again that it is never easy – at least for me, but I'm guessing it isn't that easy for the chickens either.

Well established by now is the fact that when new arrivals come to the chicken yard, we must take precautions. More complicated than simply sending out invitations to a "welcome neighbors" party, the assimilation of the new girls takes time. They must live sequestered for a time – maybe a matter of weeks; for some it is months to insure that they aren't importing diseases into the resident flock, to allow time for acclimation, and, if the new arrivals are small, to allow them to grow into "fighting" weight. They need to be able to hold their own.

And so, a separate coop, fenced off from the larger yard. The little red annex adequately, if modestly, served this purpose for time. There, the new girls get their own special feed and their own private attentions. They are close enough to grow accustomed to their nearby neighbors, and for the older ones to reciprocate, but are kept at this safe distance for everyone's well-being. This isn't, however, a country club, and eventually the new arrivals must leave their private suite.

We had been thusly tending to two young Bantam Dark Brahmas and a single Blue Wyandotte for an extended time and, determining that both precautionary objectives had been satisfied, and blessed with the fortuitous visit of my brother-in-law, who is generally game for any adventure, I divined that the time was right that night for the new girls to became full members of the sorority.

In truth, the Blue had been ready for some time, having arrived at 14 weeks of age as the replacement from the same brood as the one killed by a hawk a few weeks earlier. The Bantams, however, by definition a small version and arriving even smaller at six weeks of age, had growing to do. They seemed to appreciate the companionship of the older Blue, and so together they remained. But with their own maturity and the approach of winter, it was time. That, and a week with sparse daytime commitments on our calendar, affording a more watchful transition.

Night, then, arrived, and the great migration began. "Night," I say because there is more than one way to join a flock. I had read about these things and the strategies are many – from the callous to the careful. Having no strong conviction on the subject – I had, by this time, accomplished the move several different ways in my short history of flock keeping – I was drawn this time to a nocturnal approach. The general idea is this: since pecking order can be a sometimes violent hurdle to overcome, and since the girls become quite docile at night, take hold of the sleepy girls in their sequestered abode and manually insert them into their new destination while the already-resident girls are similarly tranquil. When the sun comes up, the older girls supposedly look over at the new arrivals and conclude, "I don't really recognize you, but you slept here so you must belong."

I don't know if anyone has actually interviewed chickens and transcribed this morning-after conclusion, but that is the general psychology.

So, under cover of darkness Steve and I made our move. Equipped with dim headlights attached to the bill of a cap, we accomplished the task; lifting each drowsing hen in turn out of her familiar roosting and then, one by one, depositing them in their new home.

Back in our home, I began to fret. I had no worries about the night. The hens sleep. All are nonplussed by the new arrangement. Morning is the concern. Amendments to the pecking order and all that; plus the fact that two of the new residents are half the size of everyone else. What was I thinking?

Morning came, I opened the hatches, the girls descended, and the usual shuffling ensued. Pecking and chasing, but less than I expected. The Blue admirably and tenaciously held her own, chest-bumping the occasional challenger. The Bantams, of course, promptly escaped the hassle by slipping through the fence and roaming the wild and unprotected yard. I understand the popular fondness for "free-range," but the vulnerability unnerved me. I maneuvered them back inside - multiple times during the course of the day.

And then dusk descended – dusk being the final vulnerability and ambiguity. Will the newcomers follow the others inside and up the ramp to bed, or feel lost, displaced and confused? It's happened both ways.

I went out to watch and discourage another escape toward more familiar roosting environs. The Blue readily followed the others up the ramp of her new home, but the Bantams paced the fence line in tandem. I stood just outside, unwittingly stepping into the theatre of time. The chickens and I respectively sensed that we straddled a demarcating line, but that line was as diaphanous as it was decisive. What lay on either side was as unknown as the nudge that would eventually carry us over it.

But whether spontaneous or considered, we were nudged. Instead of the deterrent I intended to present standing on the outside of the fence, I apparently represented something quite different. One of the Bantams, summoning all her desperate resources, took a fluttering leap to the top of the fence and then willingly into my hands, where she settled into a heart-melting and passive contentedness. We stood there for moments, the shelter and the sheltered, before I gingerly made my way inside the fence. Still I held her, until the fearful laments of her grounded partner drew her up and I set her down. Once more companioned, they again surveyed the options before taking a deep and determined breath, stepped across the threshold of their new home and, as the last of the flock, walked side by side up the ramp to bed.

I admit the lump in my throat and the tear descending my cheek - of relief? Or pride? Or, perhaps, this response did not come from my head, but from the tendered heart of the new grandfather I had recently become.

I don't know. I only know that as I walked back toward the house I felt a new appreciation for the resilience of life, the capacities for strength and courage, and the willingness to embrace the possibilities as well as the vulnerabilities of a new normal.

And I slept better that night.

And then there are those times when crises simply crawl in.

The electric fence had been cold for the past several days. "Cold" as opposed to "hot," as in not charged. I had no real explanation for this. It could be that grassy ground contact or fallen leaves or rolled hedge apples had shorted out the system. That happens with some ease and frequency. It could be that cloudy, misty days had delivered insufficient light to interest the solar charging cell. I would have to work on that. In the meantime, the chickens were "protected" by this flimsy mesh fencing. Then came the invasion.

One evening, I had headed out to the coop at dusk to close the run's outer door and was greeted by beady eyes and gray fur. It's more than a little creepy. I reviewed my early learning and confirmed that opossums are serious predators, but so far there had been no sign of aggression. The chickens allowed it wide space, but otherwise seemed unperturbed. Me? Not so much. It made me shiver. Armed with a flashlight and an egg basket I represented very little threat, but apparently the mere fact of my presence was ample incentive for the invading little marsupial to exit. Chicken feed, rather than the chickens themselves, seemed to be the extent of its appetite.

Until it wasn't. Well before dusk on a subsequent evening, I headed out back to check for eggs. Dropping the laying box trap door to see how many treasures I might collect, I was greeted by a furry white triangular face with egg yolk dripping from its chin. The little bugger had strolled into the run, made its way up the ramp and into the box and settled in for an early supper. It's one thing to be repulsed. It's another thing to be scared. It is still another to be mad. Eggs, after all, are precious!

I hustled back to the house, grabbed a sturdy broom and returned to the scene of the crime. Partially opening the rear door, I used the bristles at the end of the handle to evict the intruder through the still-opened hatch, watch it shuffle away, and then cleaned up the egg detritus so as not to traumatize the girls. After securing them inside the run, and now fueled by righteous indignation, I hopped into my pickup and headed for the farm supply store. Later, I drove back to our farmstead with a live trap and other predator control tools that will remain undefined. I baited and set the trap. Darkness fell. We turned in for the night.

We both rose early this morning – curious, anxious, horrified by the thought of what sunrise might reveal. Impatiently we tried one flashlight after another in search of an early glimpse. We were going to need a brighter light. It finally came about a half-hour later in the form of the sun which revealed – one fewer critter that the chickens and I would have to worry about. The Beverly Hillbillies' culinary mouths were no doubt jealously watering. Me? I spent the morning trying to decide if a simple benediction was adequate, or if a full-blown graveside service was required.

Such considerations have been, after all, my line of work.

The Rolling Stones once sang, "You can't always get what you want." I had no idea how true those words could be.

The day came, however, when we finally had to admit the truth - one that most objective observers would almost certainly claim to have been flatly obvious to all but the most blind or naive or self-deluded. People, in other words, precisely like us. Even we, however, finally allowed the scales to fall from our eyes. The truth? That large, strutting bird in the chicken yard sporting longer feathers and a wary attitude was not the proudly oversized hen we presumed and purchased, but a rooster. Samantha, as it turns out, was Sam despite our protests to the contrary. The "cockle-doodle-do" could not be denied.

We never intended this to happen. Our plan was to steward a quiet little flock of laying hens, fondly and appreciatively gathering each day their eggs. Roosters – cockerels – are intrusions: loud and aggressive, in more ways than one. Yes, that aggressiveness can translate into protectiveness, keeping certain predators at bay. But I had no interest in cock fighting, especially when I could be one of the contestants. I could see the sharp points on those feet and wanted nothing to do with them. And we had no interest in hatching eggs.

That, and we have neighbors I don't want annoyed each day at the crack of dawn. Neither were we, ourselves, interested in being similarly disturbed.

We did not want any roosters.

By this time, however, we had quite a lot invested in this troublesome bird – money, to be sure, and feed; but also time and attention and, dare I say it? Affection. For months we had invested ourselves in his well-being. He was one of a pair of juvenile Mottled Javas we had brought home the prior summer. We had sheltered this proud bird all this time and had grown quite attached to him, just as we had with all the other birds in our care. Although some, with a snicker, recommended various surgical procedures or suggested certain culinary recipes as solutions to our problem, we were viscerally averse to simply dispatching him - either to our kitchen or to some alternative state of being or address.

We pondered the road – and the coop – ahead, torn between what we intended, what we wanted, and what we actually possessed; needled along the way by the slightly bothersome biblical assertion that *"everything created by God is good, and nothing is to be rejected, provided it is received with thanksgiving"* (1 Timothy 4:4 NRSV).

And so it came to pass that a cock was left to cavort in our hen house. These unintended consequences happen, it occurs to me, literally and also metaphorically Maybe even politically. What to do with what I neither wanted nor intended may well turn on the degree of "thanksgiving" that Lori and I are able get our minds and hearts around.

And at what hour he chooses to crow.

We had a conversation – Sam and I. I explained about the neighbors, about our collective interest in undisturbed rest, about proper chicken yard etiquette, and that if he were to stay he would need to contribute something to the collective beyond an impressive strut. Perhaps he could look out for everyone; a "guard," so to speak.

Surprised, I have to admit, he has been quite agreeable. While he certainly takes conspicuous and aggressive interest in the hens with whom he shares living space, for the most part he pays me no mind. He accommodates my regular visits nonchalantly, preferring to supervise the feathery ones more on his level. And apparently disinterested in daybreak, our big guy delays his crow until midday. Generally speaking, his crow has been more of a suggestion than a command.

His prowess at predator control, however, leaves room for improvement.

A winter evening arrived a couple of months after Sam's true identity was revealed. It was time to close up the chickens for the night - dusk, or a little after. Fifteen minutes earlier, I had checked out the window and observed the hens still out and pecking about so I hadn't rushed. I hauled myself into an overcoat, pulled on gloves, grabbed the spotlight to check all the nooks and crannies and headed out.

I heard the commotion, but only in that vague, scratching-at-the-edges-of-consciousness way that was muffled by nearer, more preoccupying thoughts. My first real sign that something was amiss was bumping into Sam up near the front porch and heading for the yard beyond. Glancing past him I saw the girls scurrying all around the coops, at least one fully up on the roof, full of agitation. And a blur near the fence, sprinting away. As I surveyed the area with suddenly sharpened attentions I noticed first one still mound, and then another. And then another. Three dead hens. Three of my precious favorites I would later realize – a Lavender Orpington, an Ameraucana, and one of the young Bantam Dark Brahmas.

"Did you see the foxes?" a voiced interrupted. So lost in trying to assemble in my mind the reality of what had happened I hadn't noticed my neighbor approach. "We saw two in our front yard moving this way. Then we heard the commotion up here, and all the alpacas were out, looking this way."

Art joined me in the chicken yard as we surveyed the carnage and gathered up the remains. He stood watch as I secured the survivors and commiserated alongside of me. "I'm so sorry," he said softly. "I know how attached you get to them. Do you need some help carrying them?"

"Oh, I can manage," I started to respond, willing the sick taste and emotions back down my throat – and then remembered the truant rooster. "But you could help me find the rooster and get him back inside."

As it turned out, he hadn't gone far. We spotted him up near the driveway beyond the front porch. But as my neighbor and I eased behind him to encourage him back toward his enclosure it became clear that he had no interest in returning. Because he was rattled and disoriented by his own particular PTSD, the closer he came to the chicken yard, thanks to our maneuverings, the more averse he became until our only recourse was to wedge him between our crouching bodies long enough for me to grab him and forcefully carry him inside the coop – further agitating him. As well as me.

All the while my neighbor stood nearby, sympathizing, opening doors and securing gates and willingly serving as my compatriot in sadness. Together we took one last walk and look around. Finally, we snapped the gate closed behind us and paused – one last fragment of shared silence between us – and went our separate ways.

Lori and I keep reminding ourselves, whenever such sadnesses occur, that "this is nature." Though, I suspect, I will never adjust my soul to the hard truth of it, the reality is that it's not all pastoral serenity and bucolic bliss out here a few miles remote from the madding crowds; more than quietude and harvest and the daily simplicity of gathering eggs. Here in the rawness of God's order are pests and diseases in the garden and thieving birds and squirrels in the orchard. There are moles tunneling through the yard, and there are predators above and around the chicken yard attentively watching for and eventually seizing their hungry opportunity. It's beautiful out here, and serene, but the beauty and serenity are punctuated by torn feathers and blood, rot, and thorn.

Thankfully, in the midst of it all, there are also friends who appear when you need one, who stand nearby pretending not to notice the tears, who volunteer to help carry the carcasses and, from their own experiences with this hard and natural order of things, understand.

"*When you're down and troubled, and you need a helping hand...*" the lyrics spontaneously recalled, "*...you've got a friend.*"

I'm grateful, because I needed one. In more ways than one.

DRIVING HOME FROM A BRIEF WEEKEND AWAY, our house sitter called with a conundrum. There was a baby chick in our chicken coop. "What," she wondered, "should I do?" We were all baffled.

To those only superficially acquainted with our chicken interests, that phenomenon might not sound peculiar. We do, after all, have chickens. The numbers fluctuate, but our census capacity had eventually topped out at around 30. Having decided that raising baby chicks didn't fit into our lifestyle, we had made it a rule to only purchase juvenile heritage breed laying hens (excepting SamtheRooster who, as previously noted, snuck in accidentally) that are 8 weeks old or older and thusly able to live outdoors in the chicken yard rather than in our basement, in an enclosure, under a heat lamp where they are monitored every few hours, night and day.

All of which is to say that a chick in the coop, then, was an anomaly.

The fact remains, however, that we do have that rooster – a presence that comes, shall we say, with alternate potentialities.

We hurried the last few miles home and scurried out to the coop. Sure enough, there was a chick chirping loudly enough to wake the neighbors and bouncing around like a dog toy. Setting aside for a moment our disbelief, we noted that however it had gotten here it seemed to have no access to the available food and water. It was too small. Scooping it up, we prepared a temporary home for it in a box with some bedding and a lidding screen. A quick trip to the farm store afforded chick food and a waterer suitable for its size. Only then did we give our curiosity full throttle.

Could a fertilized egg have been laid and subsequently hidden for the requisite 21 days and hatched under the care of brooding hens? It hardly seemed possible. I am fastidious in the collection of eggs and tending to the coops. I'm far from perfect, but I think at some point during the course of those hypothetical weeks, I would have noticed. Alternatively, could someone be playing a prank? Could someone have surreptitiously crept into the chicken yard and deposited this fluffy ball? That seemed even less likely. None of my friends seem like practical poultry jokers. A gift from outer space? Mork in feathered form (for anyone old enough to recognize the Robin Williams reference)?

Disseminated pictures and strategic queries to hatcheries, the crowd-sourcing of FaceBook, and the DNR eventually led to the conclusion that the chick was not a chick at all, but a poult – a baby turkey; an explanation lent credibility by our sightings of a wild turkey on our property in recent days. However it came to be orphaned, and however it came to make its way inside the coop, the poult at least had an identity and a story.

What it didn't yet have was a way forward. We hadn't wakened that morning – or any other morning to date – with the aspiration to raise a turkey, and, even if the idea pricked some hypothetical nerve of appeal, we didn't know the first thing about how to go about it. For good or ill, however, we had it and it had us, together entangled in that sticky web of cuteness, circumstantial imperative, and I suppose basic nature. Whatever had caused the mother turkey to abandon her young, it simply isn't in our DNA to do the same. So it was that we found ourselves reading what we could about turkey care, exploring options for food and shelter, and saving for college.

I'm kidding about the college. But just barely.

I still don't understand it. We didn't want it; we had no interest in such things. But we had it, and came to care about it. We had hopes for it. And so, waking a mere two days later in this imposed surrogacy, when we found its lifelessly still little body nestled in the straw, we were bereft. The unclaimed had laid claim on our imaginations, our anticipations and our ever-mercurial tendernesses. On us.

We constantly remind each other that we live in the midst of nature, not Disneyland. Real things happen here. Rabbits eat the greens. Squash bugs decimate the harvest. Blight withers the tomatoes. Foxes jump the chicken fences. We have become well enough acquainted with death that I now can gather up a lifeless chicken without weeping and feeling as violated as if a thief had broken in and rummaged through the drawers. But accustomed is not the same as apathetic or indifferent. I can gather up the remains and accomplish the disposition, but every time the fact of it leaves me bruised and raw.

The sad disposition, then, even though we hadn't wanted this chirping, fluttering little bundle of fuzz in the first place.

Surprisingly, then, for the privilege of sharing this brief but tender mercy we found ourselves grateful. And we still miss the chirping little puff of adorableness.

ßß

# Chapter Eleven

# Orchard Management

*I went down to the nut orchard, to look at the blossoms of the valley,*
*to see whether the vines had budded, whether the pomegranates*
*were in bloom.*

Song of Solomon 6:11 (NRSV)

It felt a bit like horticultural cruelty. That, and flagrant, callous wastefulness.

When the kids gave me fruit trees for my birthday shortly after we moved to the farm, it was late enough in the commercial season that the nursery attendant was more interested in getting rid of inventory than dispensing guidance to an ignorant wannabe farmer. Appreciating the deep discount which enabled a larger purchase, we folded down the rear seat of the car, loaded in the young trees as delicately as possible, and delivered them to the farmstead. After amateurish reconnaissance and considered due diligence, we adopted what we hoped would be a suitable location, planted them and hoped for the best.

Though we hadn't returned home equipped with instructions from the nursery, at least the trees bore informational tags attached by a string to a branch with cursory guidance about spacing and relational needs. From the residue of science classes past and the grace of "common knowledge," we understood that some trees require companions for cross-pollination; beyond such functional necessities we surmised – or perhaps simply anthropomorphized – that the saplings might enjoy the companionship of one another. The result was a kind of neighborhood of fruit trees; intermixed, the apples and pears and apricot and plums, generously spaced according to the growing needs referenced on the tags, and yet proximate.

We were guessing, really, but accurately as it turns out. Subsequent reading of recent research described in books like *The Hidden Life of Trees* by Peter Wohlebben has attested that trees actually do communicate with one another – through pollen shared, to be sure, but more conversationally through the fungal networks underground, microscopically linking root to root, that pass along information about insect activity, disease and climate shifts. Through this arboreal party line, trees do their best to help and support each other, warn and encourage each other.

Each other, but beyond themselves as well. Diana Beresford-Kroeger notes in her beautiful book of meditations, *The Global Forest: 40 Ways Trees Can Save Us*, that "each species of tree is responsible for about forty species of insects." The ecosystem a mix of trees makes possible creates a rich biodiversity that reverberates deep and wide; in ways both apparent and invisible.

It sounds mystical and yet, as I think about it, utterly unsurprising. Knowing now what I have learned and observed about the countless reciprocities of nature, it only stands to reason. That creation is a vast coherence rather than a mixed jumble of disparate pieces and parts is evident to even a casual observer. The fact of it, nonetheless, remains a wonder to me every time I rub up against it. And a delight.

We still had much to learn. Unaddressed by the nursery sales-person and unreported on the accompanying tree tags was guidance about pruning.

When Lori and I brought home a few more trees that first spring – this time from a different nursery – the owner offered an extensive tutorial. Included in the counsel was the forewarning that the trees could possibly show fruit that first summer, but that we should prune it off to direct maximum nourishment to the roots. "This year," he offered in his best Zen voice, "the roots need all the energy."

Sure enough, springtime killing frosts notwithstanding, the trees popped with aspiring plums, pears, and apricots. I felt a first-timer's delight at the bounty and stopped to admire the fruit-ful branches every time I passed. But the nurseryman's haunting caution breathed foreboding in every rustling breeze. Indeed, I un-derstand the principle. Fruit trees – like the asparagus we had al-ready planted, and the raspberry bushes we planted that same day – are long-term investments. They aren't the peas that will move from seed to supper in a matter of weeks. Short term skimming, I know deep down, jeopardizes long term resilience and productivity. Nevertheless, it broke my heart to take the pruner in hand and do the deed. I felt like King Herod slaughtering the innocents in Mat-thew's nativity story. Or like a miscreant drowning puppies.

Helpful, then, to my conscience to come in and reread the Gospel reading for the upcoming Sunday – Jesus' metaphor about the "true vine" in John 15 in which the vine-grower not only re-moves non-bearing branches but also prunes even those branches that do bear fruit to enable them to bear still more. That charac-terization recalled my soul to the Oregon vineyards we visited one prior summer where we learned about "fruit drop" – the process of cutting out whole grape clusters so that the remaining clusters have better access to the sun, and all the vitality the vines have to offer is now concentrated rather than dissipated.

And that, of course, is the point – to encourage the best fruit the plants have to offer. Soil health, rainwater, and pruning. There was a time when I might have looked at those long-term investments and whined, "I can't wait until next year," but not this time. There is too much to look forward to in the meantime to want any of it hurrying by.

An old Chinese proverb asks:

*"What's the best time to plant a tree?*

*100 years ago.*

*What's the second best time?*

*Today."*

One of the authors I read early in the gestational stage of our new beginning – I think it was Joel Salatin – encouraged wannabe farmers, new to the land, to plant fruit and nut trees before anything else. Before unpacking the dishes, before hanging pictures, before ordering seeds for the garden, plant trees. Perhaps he, too, had learned from the Chinese. And so had we. Through the afore mentioned generosity of the kids and their birthday gift of six fruit trees, later augmented by our own hunger with several more fruit trees (along with six raspberry bushes, two blackberry bushes and fifty asparagus plants), we began our life here with the far horizon on our minds.

A time frame, to be sure, is involved. Unlike radishes and salad greens, fruit production is measured in years not days. Even the long-suffering tomato moves from blossom to ripeness in a single summer – a virtual instant by comparison. I hadn't yet studied nut trees, but I guessed that they, too, take years to mature. It makes sense, then, to plant them – if not "100 years ago," which poses an obvious problem – at least as soon as possible; the "today" to which the Chinese proverb calls secondary attention.

Something deeper, though, exposes itself to me in the wisdom of planting trees than the mere pragmatism of protracted growth. Generosity, to be sure – a down-payment on shade, as another sage voice characterized it, under which you'll not likely live long enough to sit. But with fruit trees I feel a more personal intent – an intrinsic statement of settlement. In digging the hole and lowering the root ball, I am announcing to myself, to our neighbors, or merely to God above that migratory days are past; that we are in some important sense "home"; have found a sense of place where we intend to stay. Whether or not we live long enough to enjoy its shade, we fully intend to hang around long enough to taste its fruit.

At least that message is quietly embedded in our several acts of planting for the long-term. We had no intention of living, as with the stock market, for the next quarterly report; we were investing in a life spreading out as far as we could see. Every bit as much as this land is becoming a part of us, we intended to become a part of this land – not merely for a season, but for – well – whatever time we might have left.

I cheated a little. As mentioned before and per the horticulturist's instructions, I pruned off that year's early-showing fruit in deference to sturdy roots over immediate gratification. But it so happened that I "missed" one pear. I know it was foolish whimsy. Between the birds, the winds, the bugs and the blights, the chances that we would taste its ripeness were microscopic. Still, it would grow there at least for a time – a reminder, and with any luck at all a foretaste, of the feast to come.

IT IS OUR NATURE TO LOOK AHEAD. We could argue that this tendency represents simple prudence – forethought. A likelier explanation is that the future in our imagination is typically more perfect and less work than our present. The ground around us may be mottled with weeds; the branches of the trees may be conspicuously bare, but off in the future we can be giddy with abundance.

And so it was that, long before we had any apples – or much fruit of any kind – we bought an apple press, which was its own surprising adventure. Who knew they were in such demand? When we had the idea, dreamily anticipating an abundant autumn harvest one snowy winter night in February, we wondered enthusiastically what we might do with the oversupply of fruit almost certain to inundate us some day. Cider making struck a resonant chord, and so we began to research the necessary appliances.

It turns out that cider press technology has not advanced all that far. The Internet showered us with images and descriptions of various makes and models, but they were all variations on a similar theme: a bulky caste-iron structure with a large, vertical bolt attached to a plate that is cranked down, pressing into the fruit held in some kind of a basket. Technically, it is a "fruit" press with the diverse capability of turning any number of fruit varieties into liquid. The subsequently liberated juice is squeezed through the holes or, depending on the model, the barrel staves, collected in a receptacle of one's own choosing. The model we selected was called "The Maximizer" from a retailer out of state, and after taking a deep breath at the expense of the archaic looking contraption, we thirstily began placing our order.

Imagine our surprise to discover that "The Maximizer" was on backorder. We searched out other sources. It's not that we were necessarily in a hurry. It was February, after all, and nobody would be harvesting fruit anytime soon, least of all us since our trees were only beginning to inch into adolescence. A fruit press would have exactly zero use to us for months, if not years, to come, and in fact would necessitate some serious rearrangement in the barn, should it arrive expeditiously, in order to create some place to store it. Intrigue and acquisitiveness, however, generate their own momentum. We searched, we considered alternatives; we scratched our heads at the inexplicable short supply of such a crude and uncomely device. From every source we queried the response was the same: back-ordered.

"How is it possible that there has been a run on these things?" we wondered. "Have fruit presses suddenly become faddish, and we missed the news?" Bulky, heavy, and manual; expensive and, for all its highly touted multiple fruits capability, ultimately good for only this one single application, the fruit press hardly seemed a likely candidate for a shortage. Perplexed and secretly disappointed, we nonetheless placed our order and resignedly looked forward to the distant day in July when the company anticipated the order could be satisfied.

And then promptly forgot about it, until the last week of June when a shipping notice arrived projecting delivery. Our anticipatory salivation resumed in earnest. When the truck eventually rolled to a stop in our driveway and the box was forklifted to the ground, I confirmed that the device was just as anachronistic as the pictures had suggested. The bright red paint dolled up what was otherwise a solid assemblage of welded immutability. I bolted on the accessories, attached the wheels, lubricated the bolt, and admired the quality construction, dreaming of ciders to come.

That future-tensed phrase is accurate because three years later, we still haven't pressed the press into service. I'm confident, though, that it is just a matter of time. We will certainly have the opportunity to put that advertised robust flexibility to the test since we have managed over the years to plant a diversity of fruit trees. What started with that gifted smattering of apple, pear and plum trees eventually expanded into a diverse orchard including apricots, peaches, cherries, persimmons, pawpaws, and figs; multiple varieties of apples and pears, along with hazelnuts and chestnuts — not that the latter are likely to generate much cider. We will be ready, whenever the day of the fruit arrives.

I SUPPOSE I THOUGHT THAT FRUIT TREES, once established, simply grew and fruited. In that regard, fruit trees surely share that quality of self-reliance with every other kind of tree. They simply "are" until some calamity – destructive winds, soil eroding rivers, a beaver with other ideas, or a chainsaw – causes them not to be. That, at least, is what I thought.

It is true, to an extent. Trees do seem to simply stand there with proud and aloof independence, neither asking for nor particularly wanting our interventions. Whole forests manage to perpetuate themselves with nothing but the natural resources surrounding them. Human intrusions have a way of being disruptive rather than assistive, and designed more for the benefit of those humans than the trees. I think of those poor espaliered specimens robbed of their third dimension; and those cutesy topiaries pruned into likenesses of Mickey Mouse or Dumbo or a letter of the alphabet. Who can imagine the trees' embarrassment? And stories do appear, from time to time, about long-lost orchards being rediscovered – even a single tree – bearing the sweetest fruit in memory; tended, all those forgotten years, presumably by forest nymphs or angels, if at all.

Even before our actual move to Taproot Garden, we dreamed of planting fruit trees. Apples and pears were at the forefront of our imaginations, but the fantasies, when left to drift, were more expansive. The movers had hardly driven out the driveway before we grabbed a shovel and found an earthen home for those initial six trees. True to our fantasies there were apple and pear, but also apricot and plum. We drove supportive stakes and secured the tender trunks to them. Deer, we knew, could be a hazard so we surrounded the saplings with wire cages. We watered and watched and smacked our anticipatory lips. We knew intellectually that any material harvest would be years down the road, but we could dream.

That first autumn settled into winter, which eventually thawed into spring. The discovery of buds on the infant branches brought giggles and shivers of joy. But then I dutifully if glumly pruned them away even if every snip felt like infanticide. We grieved the moment while trusting the larger good.

We continued to add trees until eventually our little orchard boasted over three dozen trees of diverse description and taste. Every year we replaced the one or two that had failed to thrive. We added drip irrigation, mulch, and thumb-twiddling patience. The more we read over the ensuing years, the more we stumbled over admonitions to manage the trees through pruning and spraying. We weren't enthusiastic. The former sounded draconian; the latter an insulting violation of our "no chemicals" determination.

But then I listened to a guest on a podcast to which I subscribed – an ordinary, non-scientific type like myself who had successfully established a community orchard in a neighborhood public park in her Canadian city. Through her ensuing trials and errors, the guest, along with her group of amateur orchardists, learned the importance of orchard management, which led to her own deeper education and eventual establishment of an online fruit tree management class. Her explanations about pruning made sense to me; the sprays she recommended were organic. Her efforts were designed to support the tree in its capacity to grow, stay healthy, and produce good fruit. I liked what I heard. Plus, "listeners to this podcast" were offered a significant discount in the cost of tuition. I went online, I entered the discount code, keyed in my credit card number, and hungrily began the first session.

Over the next several weeks I read and tested, took notes and interacted with the instructor. As tedious as it might sound, to me, it was interesting. Her horticultural philosophy and practice neatly aligned with our prior adoption of the garden principle of "feeding the soil rather than the plant." Eventually I proudly downloaded and printed my certificate of completion. I was officially a Beginning Fruit Care Manager. I was so proud.

As advertised, pruning was a major focus of the course – how, when, where, and why. I learned to recognize the difference between platform branches and scaffolding branches, the suckers and the leader branch. I learned to differentiate between blossom buds and leaf buds and to know the varied purposes of winter pruning and summer pruning. And I'll have to admit that as daunting and intimidating as was the initial idea, which made me nervous about imposing serious arboreal injury, I finished the course eager to begin.

But nature has a mind of her own – recall those calamities I referred to earlier.

Overnight and through the day freezing rain glassed the driveway and sheathed every blade and branch. Various parts of the city reported power failures from weight-broken lines, and more locally miscellaneous branches littered the yard with almost certainly more to come as the Swarovski crystal display of the moment threatens to become a horticultural holocaust tomorrow. Less of a pruning than a purge, this thinning had more in common with that lamentable fox invasion of the chicken yard that left multiple hens indiscriminately killed.

Perhaps I'm being melodramatic – I'll admit to that accusation. But nature can, indeed, be brutal. The ice was beautiful, to be sure, but the juvenile trees were fragile, and some would not withstand the assault. Nature was convening one more class session on the lesson that our human role is often less about planning and shaping and guiding along, and more about learning how to pick up the pieces and go on. Literally. Stick by stick on this occasion as it had been feather by feather in that other grizzly affair.

It prompted me to look forward to summer's drought… or would it be flood… or yet some other way the realities might intervene in the imagination? We would have to see.

Regardless, I kept my pruners handy. They would eventually be needed. Nature had taught me when to prepare; and when to repair.

ßß

CHAPTER TWELVE

# IT ALL WORKS TOGETHER

*If you want to go fast, go alone.*
*If you want to go far, go together.*

African Proverb

I grew up in a linear world. Children became adults. Education progressed from kindergarten to college. Raw materials were transformed into products, until they ultimately became trash and were hauled away. Stories and songs had a beginning, a middle, and an end. Careers moved along a similar path. With any luck, the trajectory of one's lifeline was upward, but I never questioned the perception that it was, at its core, a line. It turns out I was wrong.

Most of us are. It's not that we are devoid of lessons to the contrary. History, after all, has this thorny way of repeating itself. Over and over again. Seasons come around again. Family systems in one generation often replicate themselves in the next. We learn the same hard lessons multiple times. It may be too simple to view life as an absolute circle, but it could well resemble a Slinky, that spring toy from childhood that stretches out seemingly forever, but in a circular pattern. Just so, we learn a few things and make a little progress, but we are constantly revisiting the lessons from slightly different angles.

That's not so much a criticism as an acknowledgment about the way we learn. And, as it turns out, about the way nature thrives.

Near the time I started high school, biologist, ecologist and educator Barry Commoner published a book titled, *The Closing Circle*. I was too busy playing tennis and plucking out folk songs on a guitar to be aware of it, but Commoner was sowing seeds that would later change my life. Life, he insisted, is a circle rather than a line. Echoing ancient wisdom while, at the same time, presciently anticipating environmental consciousness that would take years to gain traction, Commoner asserted that there is no such thing as waste. In the circle of life – what he called "the remarkable continuity of life" – the detritus of one stage becomes the raw material of the next. Nature proceeds with the "reciprocal interdependence of one life process on another."

> *We have become accustomed to think of separate, singular events, each dependent upon a unique, singular cause. But in the ecosphere every effect is also a cause: an animal's waste becomes food for soil bacteria; what bacteria excrete nourishes plants; animals eat the plants. (p. 12)*

And on and on. At least that's the way it is supposed to work. Unfortunately, Commoner laments, "we have broken out of the circle of life, converting its endless cycles into man-made linear events…"

What would it look like to close the circle? What would it mean to abide by what Commoner named as the Four Laws of Ecology? Those laws as he observed them are:

Everything is connected to everything else;

Everything must go somewhere – there is no such thing as waste;

Nature knows best;

There is no such thing as a free lunch – every gain is won at some cost.

WHATEVER ELSE IT WOULD MEAN, it would mean a radical re-conception of the way we move in the world. And it would look very different. At Taproot Garden we began to be more conscious of our kitchen scraps – all those carrot tops, potato peelings, eggshells, and onion skins that once upon a time we had blithely thrown away or digested through the disposal in the kitchen sink. We began to wonder about all the spent vines and weeds that came out of the garden, suspecting that there was more that could be done with them. And what about the grass clippings and the fallen twigs and leaves and trimmed branches? Is there a way to develop and expand upon the lesson we had already learned from the alpacas next door and their generous contribution of manure?

In our readings and in the course of the myriad conferences we attended, we repeatedly encountered a word that was intriguingly new to us: permaculture. What turns out to be a hybrid word manufactured out of the root words "permanent" and "agriculture" or simply "culture," permaculture is a field of study drawn from the wisdom of nature. Although the study of it has been around much longer than Commoner's work, permaculture amplifies his Third Law of Ecology – that "nature knows best."

Grounded in the principles of "earth care, people care, and return of surplus," permaculture sits at the feet of nature, observing, listening and constantly asking, "How does nature do this?" It pays attention to interactions and movements and mutual benefits. Its design principles – for landscapes and gardens, but also organizations and neighborhoods and businesses and family systems – seek to mimic the natural ecosystems around us. "How does *this* enhance *that?*" "How would this mitigate the vulnerabilities of that?" And always, "To what beneficial use could this 'waste' be put?" My blindness to the ways nature works, my inability to see a way to generate a more sustainable method, my lack of humility to understand those gaps in the circle are disappointing signs of my own ignorance.

Our continuing education on this topic escalated to the point when, discouraged by the acrimonies and polarities epidemic in our culture and world and seeing something intrinsically healthy and hopeful in this field of inquiry, Lori signed up for an intensive, year-long course of study that would result in an international Permaculture Design Certification. In the course of her studies she learned about rainfall and runoff, in general, but also on our particular land. We procured topographical maps from the local office of the National Conservation Resource Service. She learned about wind patterns and variations in the angle of the sun depending on time of day and season of the year. She delved into beneficial plant interactions and how helpful insects were attracted and harmful ones repelled – in nature. She learned about "plant guilds" – discreet plants that in concert form ecosystems of mutual benefit.

And we experimented in the garden. I had long heard about the "three sisters," the ancient practice of indigenous peoples of planting together corn, beans, and squash. Corn is planted first so that its stalk can emerge from the ground. Beans are planted around the corn in order to use the stalks as trellis, but also because, as a nitrogen "fixer," beans return the favor by supplying corn's heavy nitrogen appetite. Finally, squash is added to the community because its large leaves shade the ground, deterring weed growth and enhancing moisture retention. The result is a mutually beneficial vegetative neighborhood.

Similarly, we experimented with companion planting in other areas of the garden – onions and peppers amidst the tomatoes; marigolds inter-planted throughout. Some of the partnerships had to do with nutrition. Some had to do with insect management.

For a practical illustration on a larger scale, we visited Stone Barns Center for Food and Agriculture in New York state, where that circle, through diligence and discovery and determined effort, is increasingly filled in. There, large animals are moved through a succession of grazing paddocks, followed by smaller animals and ultimately chickens, who scatter the manure of their predecessors while foraging food for themselves. The nourished fields are then sown for crops. The hogs that are raised in woodlots are finished in an enclosure whose bedding consists of shredded paper from the administrative offices. Once the hogs are processed, the bedding is removed to the giant compost pile adjacent to the large greenhouse, which is heated by the heat generated by the pile. The onsite restaurant, Blue Hill at Stone Barns, headed by renowned chef Dan Barber, leans heavily on the meat and vegetables raised on the property, meanwhile innovating ways to eliminate food waste from the kitchen (there rarely is food wasted on diners' plates).

Back home, we acknowledged that this whole conversation is both overwhelming and inspiring. The possible interactions and benefits among various partners playing nicely together made our head spin… in a positive way. If only the world could begin to recognize neighbors as beneficial members of a wider ecosystem, rather than threats or targets for plunder. And yet the learning curve felt overwhelming – discovering the myriad qualities and properties and considering both the negative and positive interactions each might bring to the table. It isn't quite as simple as shoving random individuals into a room and telling them to simply get along. Care must be taken. Partnerships – playmates – must be wisely chosen.

For our own continued learning – and as a concrete application for Lori's permaculture design course – we planned and planted a "food forest." A food forest seeks to mimic the routine functioning of natural forests where farmers and human "helpers" aren't required to plant and sow and weed and work. Natural forests take care of themselves. They fertilize, they plant, they prune, they renew and recycle. Modern research even suggests that they communicate among their various members. To replicate these self-sustaining systems of the forest, Lori noted the particular topography of the quarter-acre area on which we would focus. She took into consideration the "edge zones" that would provide built in boundaries – the existing woods on the north and east that would afford a wind break; the native prairie on the west that would attract pollinators; the chicken yard on the south that, in time, would supply the emergent area with natural fertilizer and bug consumption.

And then we started to plant. Lori chose cherry trees as the centerpiece, because I love cherry pies. Along with the cherries we planted peach trees, apple trees, and honeyberry bushes, because nature never plants a monoculture. But neither does nature merely plant trees. Trees – especially fruit trees – need help. I had always assumed that tree roots grew down – deep down. Some, of course, do precisely that; others, like fruit trees, create more of a horizontal sprawl. Deep rooting plants like comfrey – ones with taproots, I like to point out with a smile – are therefore planted nearby because they have the downward reach to access more remote nutrients and elevate them for the benefit of the shallower trees. Near what would be the drip line of the apple trees, we planted rhubarb and asparagus to accomplish this benefit. Immediately around the base of the trees we planted garlic chives that repel destructive insects. Nearby, we planted two varieties of asparagus. Fruit blossoms, along with the nearby pollinator flowers and the berry bushes we added, would attract the beneficials.

All that will take awhile to get established, but once mature the food forest will, indeed, look after itself. There will be food for us generated along the way – fruits and berries and asparagus and rhubarb – but their primary purpose is contributing to the plant ecosystem that is developing. Our nourishment is a fringe benefit.

It is a lot to absorb, and there are times we are tempted to willfully neglect the disciplined attentions such possibilities require. Still, this cycle of life built on mutual benefit nags and nudges us to be curiously conscious of the possible ways these same principles can be applied in the rest of our interactions. It teases and provokes our church membership, our practice of hospitality, our relationships with extended family; our marriage. Are our friendships the relational equivalents of monocultures? We convene people who all look alike, sound alike, have been formed by similar backgrounds and pull the same levers in the voting booth? Just as such uniform cropping patterns make farm life simpler, streamlining mechanization and aligning calendar schedules, mono-crop friendships make conversations easy.

But sameness is vulnerable. And static. Washing machines depend on agitation to get clothes clean. Rocks are polished the same way. Surely that is the way we grow larger and deeper as well – by the benevolent but vigorous agitation of difference that augments our own uniqueness. What are all these disparate parts assembled in a meeting room, a geographic space, or a household? What are the eccentric but valuable assets and abilities each brings to the community, and how might we come to treasure and draw vitality from our interactions? Wouldn't such societies of mutual benefit foster appreciation and grateful wonder rather than the jealousy and hoarding more commonly known? After all, sun differently shines on all those interactions depending on the circumstances, and we need the nourishment from others that we can't, from time to time, produce ourselves. We need each other – even if at any given time it isn't obvious why – or how – and so we make room and hold on.

Our Depression-era forebears, who never threw anything away, whose difficult education forged in them the recognition that everything had a future use, who learned the hard way the value of community, would smile at the prospect of us finally learning such lessons, too.

Another one of those ancient African proverbs recently popularized comes to mind: "It takes a village to raise a child." A garden, too; and a food forest; and, though we often forget the truth of it, the rest of us as well.


WE HAD WALKED THE NASCENT PRAIRIE that just days before had been burned in preparation for seeding; we had signed the agreements committing us to ongoing prairie management in exchange for cost assistance, and now the agents from the Department of Natural Resources and the Fish and Wildlife Agency were standing with me looking out over the acres. Months before we had made a similar survey. Knee-high grasses covered the expanse. "Brome grass," the agent responded when I had asked for an identification. "We probably planted it forty years ago as ground cover." Since that time Brome had fallen out of favor. Yes, it covers the ground but isn't good for much else.

The Fish and Wildlife agent made a similar observation. "You have a number of Russian olive trees on the edge of the woods surrounding the proposed prairie. We probably planted them about forty years ago as a windbreak. We quickly learned how invasive they become. We will need to cut them out or they will invade the prairie."

The two agents were offering me yet another lesson on the ways that yesterday's solutions have a pernicious way of becoming today's problems.

Months later, we stood looking past the garden we had been developing; beyond the few dozen fruit trees we had planted since moving to this plot of ground, and surveyed the three acres we were beginning to restore to native prairie grasses and pollinator wildflowers.

"When we first moved here I couldn't bring myself to dig a hole or cut a tree limb," I reflected. "It seemed arrogant to assert my vision onto the land. Now look at us."

The Fish and Wildlife agent turned his eyes from the window and addressed me with parental wisdom: "Doing nothing is also a management decision." In other words, "doing nothing is, in reality, doing something."

I know this, of course. I am not unfamiliar with children whose parents have adopted a similar "hands-off" approach. They are the dandelions of the nursery – or the classroom or the youth group or, later, the office – who contribute one annual burst of brilliant color, but otherwise displace most of the more desirable growth and quickly go to seed. Doing nothing is, indeed, doing something, producing results with generally limited appeal.

The truth is I felt some pride at the "interventions" we had made on the land. I preferred to think of them less as "impositions" than stewarding partnerships. Indeed, if the DNR's aerial photos of our property from the 1930s were any indication, the kind of work we were undertaking represented some undoing of the human interventions that had dramatically reshaped this area throughout the ensuing decades; restoration, rather than alteration. The but-terflies and bees and other pollinators so diminished in those years would once again have a habitat. That the vitality of those pollina-tors would also benefit my horticultural ambitions didn't seem too self-serving or nullifying. I rather think of it as partnership – work-ing "with" rather than "upon."

All that said, it still felt brazenly forward to cut in, cut down, dig out, burn off and plant something new in its place. And for the record, it's a lump I hope never gets easier to swallow. As I recog-nized in the very beginning of this little educational sojourn, the documents with the bank and the taxing authorities say we own this land, but we are under no such delusion. We are simply priv-ileged to live here for a time, and to do the best by it that we can.

THE BATON HAD BEEN TAPPED AND THE SYMPHONY OFFICIALLY BEGAN. The players were the seventeen-year cicadas that emerged in full force two years into our residency, and though the instrumen-tation was a bit narrow – something like an oboe on steroids – it really was quite an impressive sound. Truth be told, it was almost deafening; a wave-like undulation of varying intensities.

We had had fair warning. The media had earlier put us on alert, but I'll confess to inattention. Then, one particular and portentous Saturday morning, while walking outside with the dogs, Lori was troubled by the witness of an apparent beetle infestation of almost biblical proportions. Rushing back inside, she tore into Google Im-ages trying to identify the beetle at hand. "They are everywhere," she noted with alarm and obvious concern for the garden. Unsuc-cessful with the Internet, she nudged me outside to have a look.

Closer inspection betrayed the truth. It was true: they were everywhere. Dozens on virtually every grassy stem. According to news reports, a single tree can bear up to 40,000 – 1.5 million per acre. No wonder Lori's first concern was the garden. Plague-like, all that was missing was Cecil B. DeMille, Moses, and the Egyptian Pharaoh. Or maybe Alfred Hitchcock. Anyone the least bit arachnophobic would have readily labeled it a horror movie. But now that we recognized what they were and knew they were harmless, we could accede to closer observation – and fascination.

The "beetles" were in reality the exoskeletons from which the cicadas were emerging. Pale green and almost translucent, the newly liberated insects dried themselves on the tall grass stems, defenseless, and offered themselves up to the gods of transformation. By mid-day they had grown to a two-inch body size and found their adult colors – orange veins and big red eyes. By mid-afternoon the music had begun – the males trying their aural best to attract feminine attention. They had my sympathy. I've been to junior high dances. It's tough enough to get yourself noticed when you are simply one among a few dozen competitors. I can't imagine what it's like for the poor cicada. At least my buddies and I could try out an interesting dance move. All these guys had was a single instrument identical to the ones that everybody else in the tree was playing. Volume seemed to be the only variable virtuosity. By evening they were venturing their first flight.

They would be gone in a handful of weeks. By then we could be deaf or inured to the sound. The troops would once again march underground until their next concert in 2031. I wouldn't miss them – neither the sound, nor the concentration. Even knowing what they were and their harmlessness, the sheer numbers was creepy.

Still, it's impressive what all they go through – seventeen years underground, a climb up into the open, bursting out of a shell, drying off and stretching their wings – just to make a little music. So to speak. Good luck, little guys. I'm pulling for you.

It's difficult to travel these days. The chickens seem to think they need food and water on a regular basis and prefer to be let out in the mornings and secured at night. There are eggs to gather each day else the chickens begin to cannibalize them or they simply pile up and crack under their collective weight.

And there is, of course, the garden. Almost simultaneous with the arrival of the first seed catalogs and their glossy pictures come my visions of harvest – through ordering, garden layout, seeding in the greenhouse, planting in the rows, weeding and watering, coaxing and praying. And now, just as the picking is in full swing, comes the need to leave town. Really? Now, at the very time when a few missed seconds allows the cucumbers to swell to obscene dimensions? Now, when a neglected okra spear can morph from a culinary delicacy into a projectile that NASA could fuel and fill and launch to resupply the space station? Now, just as the squash bugs are getting out of control and the carrots are ready to pull and the tomatoes are turning red? Now?

Well, yes. Now was the time for the week-long road trip scheduled and paid for last December – before those seeds had even arrived, let alone been planted. Before we had thought about chickens or coops or the daily work of tending them.

Farming, we were quickly learning – homesteading – is not for loners.

There is ample solitude, to be sure. The chickens and I have our quiet time together. And crouched on knee pads, scooting along the garden rows with gloved hands pulling weeds and invading grass away from tender shoots and stems there is ample time to absorb the silence – or be absorbed by it. There is time and space in which to listen to your heartbeat, admire the quiet tenacity of an earthworm, glory in the butterfly and curse the nibbling varmints as though no one can hear you. Because no one will.

But farming is an act of community. No matter how self-sufficient I try to become – untethered from the conventional food system, repairing my own tools, harvesting rain, recycling manure, saving seeds, preserving harvest, cooking our own meals – we can't survive in isolation. At least not in any fashion that we would characterize as "surviving." The chickens contribute to the fertilizer, but I depend upon the alpacas next door for the bulk of it. There is always another mystery bug I need someone with more experience to identify and troubleshoot. There is equipment I can't repair.

And we like to travel every once in awhile.

We have developed relationships with a few dedicated and willing house-sitters who come and settle here during our overnight absences, tending to the dogs and the chickens and the garden and the greenhouse and whatever else comes along. Because something inevitably comes along.

In our occasional evening absence, we came to be blessed with encouraging and generous neighbors and friends who are willing stop over and pick up the slack. And the eggs. Some even hint that they enjoy it. Gary and Kay and Kathy and Art. Mike and Larry and occasional grandsons and visiting relatives who tag along or get dragged along for the novelty of seeing country life up close. And hopefully to pick a few tomatoes while they are here and fill a carton with eggs as partial payment due.

What we have learned is that we couldn't do it without them – the house-sitters and the friends. And I am grateful to them and for them – this "village" on which we depend to steward this little plot of land and its resident life.

The automated call from the water company wanted to alert me that in preparing our upcoming bill they had observed that our water usage for the ending period was significantly higher than in previous months. The message went on to encourage us to check for leaks or broken pipes.

The culprit, of course, was not faulty equipment but the beginnings of a summer unusually hot and dry. With temperatures the past few weeks in the upper 90s, uninterrupted by rain, we had indeed been supplementing the garden. Drip irrigation tapes along each row slaked the thirst of the vegetables. Emitter lines tended the fruit trees in the orchard, and the rapidly emptying rain barrels sustained the herbs and flowers nearer by. Remembering that first summer garden presided over with a garden hose in my hand, I was grateful for the simplified augmentations. It had taken weeks to flatten my hand out of the spray-nozzle shape to which it had conformed during that dry summer. These days I simply lift the hydrant handle and leave it for the requisite hours.

And pay the bill.

The bright side of this climatic inhospitality is that the grass needs less frequent attentions, and the garden weeds' reduced vigor allowed us to finally catch up to them. For the moment. Because all of this would change.

Or not.

Because this is, after all, nature not software. It twists and turns and unfolds and kinks in concert with forces outside my control and far above my understanding. Meteorologists speak of "Gulf Streams" and "El Nino" while scientists track climate change and environmental degradation. I am intrigued by their lectures and conversations, but all I really understand is that it's hot and dry and I had better pay careful attention to the leaves and the stems and the soil. There is life out there, for which I have accepted some responsibility. Gardeners can no more plant the seed and walk away than parents can deliver a child and expect it to inexorably mature.

As with most things we value – a business enterprise, an avo-cational endeavor, a relationship, parenting, peace – if we want it to thrive, indeed prosper, we can never stop paying attention; sowing, to be sure, but as often as not doing our best to receive whatever nature puts in our way…

Responding.

Adjusting.

Adapting.

Filling in the gaps.

And watering when it's dry.

It did rain a bit overnight – enough to replenish the rain bar-rels but too little to much relieve the water bill. I was grateful, none-theless, for the gift of it – and the respite.

Every little bit, after all – in life and in cultivation – helps.

WE FINALLY STOWED THE EAR PROTECTORS, looking forward to an auditory break. And a muscular one, for that matter. Having put the chain saw through its paces the past couple of weeks, we had in more recent days been encouraging the chipper/shredder to flex its muscles – and ours. And did I mention that it's loud? Once we had trimmed the cuttings and stacked them Goldilocks-style into "shredding" (the little stuff), "chipping" (the medium stuff) and "burning" (the big stuff), we pulled the starter rope, affixed the eye and ear protectors as the 14-horse engine roared to life, and started feeding the beast.

There would prove to be more chain-sawing necessary, short-ening a few of the larger limbs that had escaped notice to make them more suitable for the fire pit, but, otherwise, the piles grad-ually diminished. And it felt good – partly to have several of the trees in better trim, and partly just to have the project completed for a time and cleaned up. But what felt especially good was having the limbs turned back around for their next contribution. In the coming months, the wood chips would become mulch around the bushes and flowering trees in the meadow to help initially with moisture retention, and later, as the chips work their way into the soil, as organic matter rebuilding the soil to support the growth of new limbs that will eventually be pruned and chipped and mulched all over again. It's nature's "right and left grand" around the circle of life before returning home.

And it's one of the lessons we have been trying to practice from nature's way of farming: that there is no such thing as waste. The end-put of one process – trimmed and shredded branches, animal manure, egg shells, food scraps, etc. – becomes the valuable input of another. "Waste," as commonly understood, is less an indictment of the unappreciated material at hand than it is of my lack of understanding and underdeveloped imagination. Waste is simply that which I haven't yet discerned how to beneficially use.

But we keep learning and exploring and experimenting. The kitchen scraps that the chickens can't eat we compost. The grass clippings and leaves I once bagged and hauled away get the same composting treatment. The straw bales – "waste" from someone else's field – stacked in winter around and insulating the chicken coops eventually, come springtime after a winter of weathering and manuring, get spread over the potato beds among other things to protect and nourish a new season of growth. And then become organic matter worked into the soil.

The circle of life. A kind of barn dance with a "right and left grand."

If only the idea would catch on in other parts of life.

More appreciation than judgment.

More creativity than disposal.

More integration than isolation.

Respectful welcome of the intrinsic possibilities, rather than dismissive rejection of the richness undiscerned.

Who knows how fruitful we might become?

We might even begin bowing not only to our partners, but to our corners as well; and dancing – promenading – along with the rest of creation.

# Chapter Thirteen

# Trials and Errors

*God saw everything that he had made, and indeed,*
*it was very good.*

(Genesis 1:31 NRSV)

It couldn't be any simpler. Order some seeds, identify where you want them to grow, prepare the soil, sow, water and wait. Voila, supper!

Except that it turns out it isn't quite that simple. Seed packets generally describe what the seeds inside require – depth of planting, days to germination, days to maturity. They also indicate whether the seed should be started indoors and then transplanted or planted directly into the garden soil. A few plants aren't suitable for transplanting, but most are happy either way.

I understood the need to start certain long-growing varieties early – peppers, for example, and tomatoes. Our growing season isn't long enough to start such seeds in early spring and hope to gather a harvest. But in the beginning I couldn't imagine why anyone would willingly opt to employ two motions – starting in the greenhouse and then transplanting them later in the garden – rather than one if seasonal constraints didn't require it. Gardening is demanding enough as it is. Why complicate the matter? Let the sowing begin!

Using a fancy software I had downloaded, I mapped out the garden space – framing the perimeter, drawing out the planting rows and then dragging and dropping into the design where each varietal would go. I clicked "save," sat back in my chair and admired the virtual design. Beautiful! Already my mouth was watering.

Spring arrived, and eventually the threat passed of even a late frost. I set about translating my computerized design into actual soil and beds. Methodically I distributed the seed packets around the garden according to the design and set about the meticulous process of introducing the contents to their respective neighbor-hoods. Seed spacing was a factor I hadn't much considered; after all, nature doesn't have a yard stick to methodically apportion its progeny. Nevertheless, I honored the packet instructions to the best of my ability. One foot apart. An inch apart. Spinach requires less space. Broccoli more. It took tedious time, but I humbly acknowl-edged that whoever had written the instructions could only know more about it than I did. I bowed to her or his expertise.

Transplanting seedlings is even more satisfying. You can in-stantly see the row come to life. Tender stems, spare but determined leaves, ordered – even inspirational promise. Beautiful!

The sight of a freshly sown garden is nourishing in itself. There is an honesty about it – an earthy richness and beauty. Dark soil, neat rows, the almost perceptible vibration of promise, the mystery of growth. I finished the work and stood silently at the gate, letting the wonder of it – the exhilaration of actualized dreams, the sat-isfaction of observable accomplishment, the goodness of my own physical fatigue – encircle and buoy me. Beautiful!

I was smiling as I closed the gate, put away the tools and nudged my weary, soil-smudged self toward the house.

Perhaps it wasn't quite the next morning, but it wasn't very many mornings later that my bucolic attitude faded. I had planted vegetable seeds, but it turns out they weren't alone. Soil, as mentioned earlier, is crowded with life, and that life wills to emerge. Nature, I've come to learn, abhors bare ground and will do just about anything to cover it. Its first line of attack is weeds. Seeds are designed to grow, but weed seeds are, perversely, designed to grow faster. And they are prolific. Long before the emergence of whatever vegetable had been intended in a given space, miscellaneous other stems quickly appear; and that creates a problem for a novice like me. It wasn't any resistance to working a hoe; I was prepared for that. The problem was identification, or perhaps discrimination.

I stood at the edge of the garden and leaned on my hoe, staring at the random spots of green. Where to start – and on what plant? Never having grown such things before, I had no frame of reference from which to differentiate ragweed from cabbage, crabgrass from spinach, dandelion from collard. Everything looked the same, at least to eyes like mine more accustomed to identifying typographical errors than horticultural miscreants. I was paralyzed by my inability to separate what belonged from what was in the way.

I thought of the biblical parable about the futility of separating the wheat from the tares and opted to take the biblical way out. The truth would eventually become evident and then I could take remedial action.

Alas, a few weeks later, when the "spinach" proved to be merely grass and the "carrots" yet more dandelions I realized that my biblicism had exacted a terrible price. By this point the interlopers had gained an indefatigable upper hand. Definitely not beautiful!

THE OLD ADAGE SUGGESTS THAT WEEDS ARE SIMPLY PLANTS growing where you don't want them to be. With the garden fully planted that first season, with growth actively underway, I began discovering the dubious companionship of all sorts of these "plants growing where I don't want them to be." Indeed, I found that the name chosen for our humble effort – "Taproot Garden" – was coming back to haunt me, with many of these inconveniently located plants establishing a prior claim via impressive taproots of their own. The above ground portion of one such specimen measured perhaps a foot in length, while the taproot shot down into the ground fully half again that length – at least the portion of it I extracted. A close inspection of the tip revealed a truncation likely to be the foretelling of a growth-ful return.

Every day, this tedious business of uprooting humbles me. It has never been lost on me that I am the interloper exerting an alternative point of view, an alternative rigor, and an alternative desired outcome than simply the fullness of growth and spread as intended by these... er... uh... "weeds." They were here first, stretching their whiskery toes and gleaming torsos in opposite directions to reciprocal benefit. And by the looks of the landscape, they have been doing so happily and with wildly successful results for some time.

I am under no delusion as to my own effectiveness. A scant few weeks of inattention, I knew full well, and that garden space I so laboriously carved out of the acreage would be utterly reclaimed and reversed. These are the truer inhabitants of "Taproot Garden"; merely and begrudgingly allowing me temporary use. Long after I am finished and moved on, they will be thriving in place; the wounds of my tiller and spade long erased and forgotten.

It's a sobering discernment, but worth holding before me lest I lose myself in the hubris of cultivation. The flimsy little fencing I stretch around the rows for protection no doubt does little more in the long run than allow me a season's night sleep; it doesn't ultimately stake much of a claim – nor do I. Mother Earth will have her way.

Maybe this sort of cautionary reminder of transience is what scripture intended when it observed that we are dust, and to dust we shall return; grass that flourishes for a time and then withers.

Who knew that arrogance could be blunted by a little simple weeding?

SEVERAL MENTIONS HAVE BEEN MADE OF A "GREENHOUSE." From the beginning we assumed we would need a greenhouse. We didn't have any clear picture of what such a structure might look like on our property, but, as far as my ignorance could discern, shelves would be as essential as soil. And lights. Underscoring the importance of such an incubator, our early experience with direct seeding and battling competing weeds quickly eroded my aversion to the idea of transplanting. We had inherited a cement pad on the south side of the barn; residue, I supposed, of a dog kennel. It wasn't large – perhaps 8-feet by 10-feet – but it was conveniently located and seemed well suited to floor the structure taking shape in my mind. I wasn't sure why a greenhouse needed a cement floor, but we had one and it sounded nice. A nearby electrical outlet on the side of the barn made the location still more desirable. At least it was a place to start.

Very few computer key strokes landed me in the midst of a burgeoning online marketplace devoted to structures for growing. Some were vast, bent steel beam structures variously called "hoop houses" or "high tunnels" skinned with plastic film enclosing thousands of square feet. There were glass ones, wood-framed, windowed buildings; huts the size of a dog house, cold frames on the ground, porch covers for the house, with all designs available in every shape and size. My head was swimming with so many options, churned by a complete ignorance of what rationale I should employ to sift the variables. I read descriptions. I read reviews. I winced at the cost. Ultimately, I made a calculated judgment, entered my credit card number, closed my eyes, and pressed "complete purchase."

The model I chose, roughly sized to fit my concrete pad, consisted of PVC and composite poles to form the skeleton, covered by a plastic material called "Solexx." Similar to corrugated cardboard, Solexx is a double-walled plastic sheeting, about a quarter-inch thick that is screwed onto the building frame. Milky-white, the material is designed to be durable, diffuse the light, provide modest temperature control, and be relatively simple to work with. That last feature was especially appealing to me.

Like so many other elements of this new adventure, I hadn't really thought through how the greenhouse would arrive. It wasn't that large, after all; surely it would arrive on a trailer, ready to off-load and admire. Hardly.

When I was a child I used to watch a cartoon chronicling the daily life of a space-aged family named the Jetsons. The show featured video phones, moving sidewalks, a robotic housekeeper named Rosie who prepared reconstituted freeze-dried and encapsulated meals in an instant, and flying cars. I especially marveled at the flying cars, and giggled at the way George Jetson's car collapsed into a suitcase when he arrived home each evening, a suitcase small enough that he carried it inside and tucked it into the closet.

I thought of that briefcased car when the eagerly anticipated greenhouse arrived. Only slightly larger than George's briefcase, the couple of boxes delivered to our driveway bore frighteningly little resemblance to a structure. A large, thin box contained the sheets of Solexx. Another, smaller one contained the hodgepodge of PVC poles, straps, and two gallon-size freezer bags swelled to capacity by one-inch screws. Oh, and a flyer with assembly instructions. I almost wept. "Some Assembly Required" are the three most terrifying words in my vocabulary. Screwdrivers, hammers, and drills don't fit naturally in my hands, more accustomed as they are to handling pens, keyboards, and guitars – and now a hoe and hose.

Fortunately, we have friends – one of whom, in particular, loves this very kind of challenge. Larry and Shirley – the ones who had generously offered me the use of their land to practice garden a few years prior – are innovative problem solvers, unafraid of any technical, logistical, or mechanical challenge. They happily throw themselves into monumental projects that would daunt even the most seasoned tradesman, and, as I mentioned before, are incredibly generous. I called them and dangled the immensity of the undertaking in front of me. Immediately recognizing the impossibility of my predicament, they enthusiastically replied, "Sure. We'd be glad to help."

"Help," of course, is a laughably dishonest description. I was the one who helped. They were the project managers, chief engineers, master instruction interpreters, and work horses. My primary contributions were carrying, lifting, handing, retrieving. I eventually took hold of the power driver to reduce that mountain of screws, but it frequently took more than one attempt to get them in the right place and at the correct angle. Over the next few weeks a structure gradually arose over the slab. Intense work days ensued, a few short ones, some profane ones in which everything seemed to go wrong, and even a couple in which work progress was periodically interrupted by a feverish Larry slipping away into the nearby woods to be sick before returning to the project he was determined to see finished.

As the temperatures and last leaves of autumn dropped and the first hints of winter chill rustled the bare branches, we secured the door, tested the latch, christened the completed project, and smiled. A marvel, in more ways than one.

Looking back, I shudder at the naïveté of my purchase. There is no way the contents of that inconspicuous pair of boxes could have ever been transformed into a useable structure by any efforts the two of us homesteaders could have marshaled. If, as I and the old African proverb have noted, it takes a village to raise a child, it takes good, charitable and long-suffering friends to raise a greenhouse. And I am forever grateful – for their friendship, and for the fact that the friendship survived the project.


I SUPPOSE THERE IS NOTHING MORE NATURAL IN THE WORLD than seeds germinating and eventually bearing fruit. That's what seeds do: through one means or another – a soft landing, a bird, an animal or a cooperative farmer – they find a habitable place to nestle in and turn their built-in creative energies loose. It has been happening since Eden. It just didn't happen so readily or reliably at Taproot Garden.

With our greenhouse proudly assembled, the closing weeks of winter still holding us otherwise captive, we convened a wide assortment of plastic seeding trays, purchased bags of potting mixture, and busily set ourselves to the task of nudging this age-old process into motion. A small space heater that we hoped would keep the interior climate somewhere south of the arctic was plugged in and switched on. An obligatory watering can was filled and situated inside. Shop lights were affixed above to stretch the sunlight. Thusly warmed, watered, and lighted, we waited.

And waited. Yes, there were sprouts – here and there. There were tantalizing natal glimpses of thin green wisps and tiny leaf-like protuberances I would later learn are called cotyledons that, if we were so fortunate, would eventually be replaced by "true leaves."

The disappointment was that there simply weren't very many. A 72-cell tray might only have 10 cells that betrayed signs of life. Some had more; some had none at all. We would have plants, in the end, but hardly reflecting our investment in seeds. Something was clearly missing.

The following year we changed our starting mix, switching to an organic compost-based product we had learned about at a conference. It helped, but our success rate still disappointed us – only improving to 40 to 50 percent. By this time, we were storing rain water in our garage through the winter that had been collected in rain barrels throughout the autumn, using it exclusively in the greenhouse, and clearly the seeds preferred the purer drink. At half germination, however, we slipped into the practice of significantly over seeding; assuming a poor return.

We learned a little more and made a few more changes. Soil temperature turns out to be more important than air temperature, and so we added heat mats beneath the trays. We also wearied of the flimsy seed trays and switched over to making our own soil blocks using a tool that creates a dozen soil "brownies" at a time with a neat dimple in the center just waiting for a seed. Creating the blocks is time and labor intensive, but there is also something satisfying about mixing the soil with water to the right consistency, stamping out a dozen blocks at a time, placing and covering the seeds and nestling the blocks onto the heat mats. The blocks do a better job of hosting and encouraging the seed and, when spring arrives, are transplanted in their entirety into the garden.

The results were wonderful – in a terrible way. Almost 100 percent of the seeds germinated. That is almost 100 percent of our over-planted seeds. Suddenly we had a crowded forest in the green-house. "Be patient," we cautioned ourselves. "Not everything will thrive." But almost every plant did. Our nursery was teeming with horticultural children, and by garden time – and after the prior seasons of meagerness – we couldn't bear the thought of abandoning any of them.

And so, we made room. Somehow. Inevitably some resulting rows were overcrowded. We tilled up new spaces. We wedged them all in. And quietly nursed conflicting hopes that all would thrive – or wouldn't.

We have gotten better over the years. We no longer assume the worst and have tempered our sowing. Slightly. But between our residual caution, our reticence to squander any of the seeds in a packet, and our fascination with a multiplicity of varieties – nine or sometimes ten kinds of tomatoes; six or seven varieties of peppers; green cabbages but also red, and so on – we still approach transplant time with a preposterous number of plants for two people to tend, harvest, and consume. Any given year is likely to see upwards of 150 tomato plants of one kind or another. It's madness really, but a joyful madness. The absurd abundance has prompted us to learn an expanding repertoire of preservation tactics. Canning salsa, of course, was an obvious starting place for a transplanted Texan with an insatiable appetite for Mexican food. But even I couldn't consume that much salsa. We expanded to homemade ketchup, Italian marinara, tomato paste and tomato juice, barbecue sauce, and even pickled tomatoes. Tomato paste, in particular, is an impressive way to use up an excess harvest: start with a wheel-barrow load of tomatoes and end up with a tablespoon of paste. It's amazing. In recent years we have turned to dehydration as a way to conserve storage space and vary the options. But still there are too many. And we love it.

We discovered fermentation while addressing an overabundance of cabbage. Now, we are constantly on the watch for innovative uses of sauerkraut. Or household favorite is the Reuben pizza

– a flattened and baked knock-off of the familiar sandwich. All in all, between our freezers and the pantry shelves, we don't spend much time at the grocery store.

And every year we tell ourselves that we aren't going to plant as much this season. One of these days that might actually happen.


Ann Patchett once wrote, "Never be so focused on what you're looking for that you overlook the thing you actually find." She could have been writing about a garden.

Weeding eventually becomes an assumption rather than an interruption, at least in a garden managed organically. I recognize that there are chemicals to control such invasions, easing the burden, but we eschewed the use of such toxins early on in our imagination and then in our cultivation. There are differences of opinion on this subject – militantly defended opinions – and while it is true that the vast majority of fruits and vegetables consumed in this country are grown with a steady shower of herbicides and pesticides, we've opted for the more natural route. Hence, the hoe.

We have improved with experience and practice, pulling some, blading others, preventing what is reasonable. Our tool shed is a bloated hodgepodge of short handles and long handles, the favorites and the forsaken. I'm a sucker for any wood and metallic innovation that purports to simplify the labor. Recently, however, we transitioned our growing system from trenches to raised beds created by a two-wheeled walk behind tractor with an ingenious array of interchangeable implements that simplify the "construction." In the process of making the switch, a lot of dirt was moved around, and apparently some dormant weed seeds. Magically, it seemed, something new appeared.

I say it was new. I can only confirm that I had never noticed it before. If it plagued our garden in previous years I hadn't see it – or

I was consumed with different, more urgent concerns. Suddenly, this season, it seemed to be everywhere. And very, very happy. One of the new sections of the garden was particularly afflicted. Daily, I ran the wheel hoe through the walking spaces and between the plants, clearing the overgrowth, and by morning the ground would be covered again as if I had been absent a week. Blast this low-growing, oddly attractive, curiously prolific succulent.

Providentially, an acquaintance who operates a certified organic vegetable farm in the area, came over to perform an annual inspection to renew our Certified Naturally Grown designation for garden and chickens. Passing through the garden gate I pointed out this spidery green nemesis, muttered a few profanities by way of description, and asked if he had any idea what it is. His lips curling into a knowing, sympathetic smile, he uttered a single word: "purslane."

I had heard of purslane, and been curious about it, but obviously had no idea what it was. The Internet offers plenty of pictures, of course, but scale is difficult for me to assess in such photos, and I'm left never really sure of what I'm looking for. The mystery, however, was suddenly solved. "It's edible," my inspector friend elaborated, and went on to tell me that most other cultures value the plant's culinary and nutritional assets. We, on the other hand, cavalierly label it a weed and hoe it away. Together we plucked some leaves and sampled some of this aspirational supper. "Not bad," I thought as I considered the possibilities.

Later, having chewed a few more leaves after my friend departed, we researched for more understanding. I had already discovered the desultory fact that nature abhors bare ground. It isn't cosmic peevishness. It is care-taking. Bare ground rapidly loses moisture. Bare ground blows away. So, it is that Nature finds ways to cover it. Quickly. Enter: purslane. But as my organic friend had hinted,

Nature isn't the plant's only admirer. Purslane is a wonder inside the home as well. Indeed, enjoyed around the world, the plant, some believe, originated in Persia and India. Italians have included it in their favorite recipes since the 1200's. Sporting higher levels of Omega-3 fatty acids than many fish oils, impressive levels of fiber, vitamin A, vitamin C, B-family vitamins, iron, magnesium, potassium, calcium, copper, antioxidants and carotenoids, this pesky yet delicious little weed can reduce "bad" cholesterol, reduce cardiovascular disease, assist in weight loss, prevent certain cancers, boost vision, strengthen the immune system, build strong bones and improve circulation. Where has this stuff been all my life?

In her book, *The Wild Wisdom of Weeds*, Katrina Blair delivers kitchen recipes for Purslane Sauerkraut, Walnut Purslane Coleslaw, Purslane Peach Pie, Purslane Lime Sorbet and Purslane Gazpacho among others. Hygienically, she walks readers through the steps to Purslane Lemon Elixer, Purslane Shampoo and Purslane Lotion.

I'll have to admit that, while I'm becoming more and more adventurous in the kitchen, I'm skeptical as to how many of those "weeds" are going to show up in our culinary repertoire. Nonetheless, I'm excited to try something new – ancient, that is, but new. Happy, as well, to approach my weeding with a kinder, more benevolent view.

This curious little succulent has also given me broader pause. It couldn't hurt to approach a few other things in my world with those clearer, more informed eyes as well – wondering what other "purslanes" might be out there in the neighborhood, in the communities through which I pass, in the various immigrant communities to which we all belong; things and people who look, for all the world, like weeds but could just save our lives.

It's at least something to chew on.

NOTE TO SELF: It doesn't all have to look the same.

Truthfully, I'm a little embarrassed. Throughout the generalities of my adulthood and the particularities of my ministry, I have fought against the cultural curse of homogeneity – the bigotries that lead otherwise decent people to marginalize, demonize, and even fear those who don't look, pray, talk, or parse gender identity the same way they do. Such xenophobia underlies some of the bleakest chapters in our human history, from the many examples of slavery, to the Inquisition and the Holocaust, and to the far less visible but no less shameful treatment of farm laborers. Some would argue that most of these examples are more economic than social. Money undoubtedly plays a role, but I would counter that we simply could not treat these victims with such brutal and dismissive disregard if we truly viewed them as equally human. Our pattern with each other is coldly clear: those we despise, labeling them "weeds," we either subjugate or annihilate. And mostly, if history bears witness, what we despise is anyone we perceive to be "different."

In farming, the rationale is different, but the result is the same. More and more, we homogenize. And this, too, betrays an irony that embarrasses me. For some time, I have saluted the red flags raised by those journalists and agronomists concerned about the vast mono-crops that have become modern agriculture – whole fields of nothing but broccoli; entire counties of corn; oceans of tomatoes; vast landscapes of sameness. These mono-cultures cater to simplicity rather than nutrition, mechanization rather than human labor, and portability rather than flavor. And because of intrinsic vulnerabilities to particular pests and diseases, they are built upon a steady diet of pesticides and herbicides and genetic modification rather than natural, organic practices and treatments. The best environment for healthy and happy vegetables (and the people who consume them) is a poly-culture of multiple varieties, growing in close proximity, nourishing and protecting each other.

I know these things, believe these things, and teach these things at every opportunity. Mono-cultures – within the garden or the community – are dangerous and sadly impoverished. Poly-cultures – many different types, growing and thriving side by side – are more interesting, more nourishing, and ultimately more secure.

Why is it, then, that in our garden I have sought such pristine perfection in the pathways between the garden rows? Why is it that I have so maniacally worked to eradicate the clovers and the Queen Anne's Lace and the myriad other growing things that diversify the spaces outside the growing areas? How is it that I came to wield such antagonistic force as to break two weeding tools in pursuit of my self-defined purity? Who knew that I had such a virulent inner Nazi determined to propagate a perfect race of turf at the expense of anything that didn't fit into my horticultural stereotype?

It could, I suppose, be construed that with this sermon I am simply admitting defeat – implicitly acknowledging that the "weeds" have gotten the best of me; that I will never succeed in their eradication, and that I am providing myself with a convenient philosophical – yea, verily, *moral* – rationale to cover my retreat.

But I don't think so. What I believe is that our corruptions and misunderstandings are deeper and subtler than we like to admit. In the face of such intransigence, truth comes to us along its own path, in its own time – like water finding cracks and seeping inside. And the truth is that it doesn't all have to look the same. Truth, and its intimate companion, "wisdom." Some things can be taught; others, like seeds, must moisten and crack open to allow the fragile tendrils of growth to root themselves into healthier, more expansive soils.

I am embarrassed by the time it took for this particular seed to break open in me, and all the gardening energies misspent in a pointless pursuit. The vegetables, patiently forgiving of such squandered time, will nevertheless be thrilled with my new attentions.

I SUPPOSE IT GOES WITHOUT SAYING that it is hard to see what you can't see.

Back in May of that first garden season, I planted three types of potatoes: French Fingerling, left over from last season; Yukon Gold purchased at the local farm store, and basic Russets, gone to sprout in my mother-in-law's garage. I cleared the trenches, scattered in the seed potatoes, covered, and waited. Along the way, they actually sprouted (I continue to be surprised by such things), blossomed, and, well, that's the mysterious part. After the blossoms, it's hard to know exactly what else might be going on beneath the surface.

On faith, then, I weeded and watered and watched and waited. Eventually, late in the summer, I had thought to dig them up, believing – for reasons I can't quite put my finger on – that it was "time." I was supposed to have help on the day I planned the digging, but that fell through. No worries, however. I rather enjoyed the discovery process, and it didn't turn out to be that much work.

Which is a coy way of saying there weren't that many potatoes to find.

I started with the Fingerlings; pitch-fork loosening the soil, then hands and knees and fingers making my way along the trench. I will say this: if there were an award at the State Fair for the smallest potato, a blue ribbon would be in my future. There were certainly nice sized ones, but my heavy harvest in this category that year was less the size of the eponymous finger and more along the dimensions of the lentil – half a dozen or so to the mouthful.

On to the Yukon Gold, where results were a little more impressive – golden golf ball-sized ones, along with others slightly smaller, unearthed in this partial trench abutting the now-vacated garlic bed.

To be sure, I had the least invested in the Russets, which turned out to be a good thing. They were the most disappointing producers – the harvest barely replacing the eyed chunks I had buried in the beginning.

More reading would be required on the finer art of potato cultivation, despite the "any boob can grow potatoes" reassurance proffered by my preliminary inquiries. This boob's efforts would barely rate a C- by any objective assessment, although the 15 pounds or so I weighed in with isn't a total embarrassment. Besides, they made up in taste what they lacked in volume.

Around that time a memory resurfaced of a passage I had read in a book about results.

> *To be a greedy gardener seems somehow offensive. What I get from the garden I like to regard as a gift. Nature and I have cooperated. Though when we have summers of drought, then summers when it rains daily for six weeks and the garden is a swamp, I feel angry, cheated. Who's cooperating here? This is my garden! Not my chief source of food, it's true, but the food I most covet and hoard in the deep freeze for the worst of winter nights, an essential ingredient of the life we've made for ourselves here.* (Deborah Tall, *From Where We Stand: Recovering a Sense of Place*, p. 150.)

SLEEPING ON MY DESULTORY FEELINGS regarding my underwhelming potato harvest, I rose the next morning feeling the need to repent. Tall is right in her observation: greed in a gardener is, indeed, offensive. That anything emerges at all – meager or abundant – is, indeed, a gift. Especially for me. If this garden is a cooperative effort between Nature and me, then I can only acknowledge receiving the more enviable share. Nature, in my helping hands, gets the shorter end of the bargain. True, I am attentive – to a fault. True, I am protective. True, I am eager to learn. But this latter is an extraction rather than a contributive asset. It carries within it the hope of future capacities. But speculative tomorrows offer little consolation to the deficits aching today.

Grace, then, anything this garden manages to deliver – gift and grace. So, I recant my tomato critiques and potato belittlements; recant, as well, my disparagements of the collards' slow pace and the beets' indifference to my schedule. They are all alive and growing and offering up something of themselves, even if it's not what I pictured in the dead of winter from the comfort of my recliner. Their capacity to survive at all in the worst heat and drought in decades – along with my clumsy ministrations – should, if anything, inspire wonderment and awe, rather than this gratitude squeezed with as much parsimony as I have accused the garden itself of offering.

So, yet another lesson learned. This is real life, not the glossy photographs in the seed catalogs. And however uneven the partnership, Nature and I are cooperating. Tilling up the now-empty potato trenches and scattering in a few more leftover seeds, I resolved to let the partnership continue.

And come that "worst of winter nights" when I reach into the deep freeze – or the shelf of canned produce – what I touch will be the food I most covet and hoard, not simply for the gift of it, but for the miracle of it existing at all.

Truly a blessed and "essential ingredient of the life we've made for ourselves here" (Deborah Tall).

*The principal value of a private garden is not understood. It is not to give the possessor vegetables and fruit (that can be better and cheaper done by the market gardeners), but to teach him patience and philosophy, and the higher virtues, – hope deferred, and expectations blighted, leading directly to resignation, and sometimes to alienation. The garden thus becomes a moral agent, a test of character, as it was in the beginning. I mean to have a moral garden, if it is not a productive one, – one that shall teach... the great lessons of life.* (Charles Dudley Warner, *My Summer in a Garden,* 1870.)

I must confess that I began with somewhat lower expectations. I simply wanted to learn about growing food. Like death and dying, this central element of living has moved away from home for most of us, to the "experts" who handle such things on behalf of the rest of us. Sensing that we lose something precious in this removal, I resolved to do something about the agricultural aspect, if not quite so immediately the funereal.

Along the way, however, the garden expanded its curriculum, becoming a multifaceted classroom for the heart and soul as well as the mind and stomach. Lessons in patience I expected – gratification delayed – but "hope deferred" caught me by surprise. It had not come to "resignation" or "alienation," although more than a few expectations have been "blighted," as those first seasons neared their completion. I had not thought too much of Eden in the context of my humble enclosure of furrows and trellised vines, but as with that first one my little garden occupied its space as an active moral agent and test of character, touching on more than a few sage nuggets.

Vegetables, for example, don't have to be "grocery store perfect." One night in those latter days of the first season we sautéed some Swiss chard that bugs had Swiss cheesed with holes. It wasn't, perhaps, photographable, but it was delicious. I quickly lost count of the BLTs we enjoyed, built around cracked tomatoes.

And as for that "hope deferred"? Patience, as it turns out, really became everything. Among the seedlings in the greenhouse, the brassicas were the first to sprout – hardy delights like kohlrabi, cabbage, broccoli and kale. The kohlrabi was the first to emerge. The purple cabbage was a close second. Healthy and eager, I transplanted them in May with high expectations and relative confidence. The rabbits, of course, matched their eagerness and, as far as I could tell, demolished them. A few pathetic twigs remained here and there, and I didn't have the heart to till them under, but they remained as sad altars to dashed dreams.

Now at the birth of September - months after most had harvested their brassicas – mine had rejuvenated themselves, almost flaunting their promise. The stalks were proud. The foliage, majestic. The resurrected plants were beautiful. Maybe Churchill was right in 1941: "Never give in – never, never, never, never, in nothing great or small, large or petty, never give in except to convictions of honor and good sense. Never yield to force; never yield to the apparently overwhelming might of the enemy." I recognize that the evil of which he spoke was somewhat larger than hungry rabbits, but the point remained.

And so, my gratitude swelled for all that steadily and surprisingly happened in the little "schoolhouse" behind our house – all it was teaching, and all I struggled to learn. The Brussels sprouts still haven't shown themselves, but who could predict? Anything was possible. And if worse came to worse and we had to survive without them – well, I am sure there are more horrible fates. We'll at least have beauty.

PROGRESS WAS SLOW, BUT DISCERNIBLE. Anyone who has known me through the years knows that I am a word guy. I'm not a math guy; numbers make my head go numb. I'm not an art guy; my stick figures don't even look like stick figures. And I am definitely not an equipment guy. True, I like my gadgets as well as the next guy, but most sensible people start reaching for hardhats and storm cellars whenever I pick up a power tool. And that's just with me trying to use them. The world clock ticks one minute closer to midnight anytime I give a thought to actually trying to repair one.

But here we were out in the country – homesteading after a fashion – where it rapidly became evident that equipment was a prerequisite. That, or perhaps it was my gadget fascination let off its leash. Power equipment.

Horsepower.

Gasoline.

Diesel.

Gas/oil mix.

Even more than a few things that plug in.

Mowers, blowers, tillers, haulers, trimmers, chippers, chainsaws, compressors.

A friend repeatedly called attention to my steadily rising "cylinder count."

And here is something I gravely came to notice: all of these gadgets can malfunction, go flat, get dull, get clogged, or simply break. What's a "word guy" to do – other than mutter a few blue ones?

When we first moved out here I called people when the unexpected happened – friends, neighbors, repair shops… Sometimes these interventions involved people coming here; sometimes it involved me taking something there. Friends were generous, but eventually began to screen my calls. And repair people, once they finished laughing, usually had this frustrating expectation of being paid for their services. So, what's a "word guy" with a diminishing pool of friends and a diminishing savings account to do?

Even at the risk of global annihilation, I began taking several deep breaths and trying to fix things myself. When the chain saw chain slipped off one Friday evening I initially set it in the back end of the pickup until the following Monday when I could take it in to the shop. And then I thought about all I needed to get sawed and took a closer look. Unfathomably, I got it back together. One of the wheelbarrow tires went flat and, firing up the air compressor, I actually restored its roll without blowing myself up. Eventually I managed to attach the snowblower to the tractor without the coddling assistance of friends, and when spring reappeared I managed to detach the snowblower and replace it with the mowing deck, again all by myself.

But the day arrived when I found myself once again against a wall. More literally, I found myself almost against a tree. Over the course of a few weeks we had experienced Noah-like rains, making it difficult to mow. Either the sky was pouring or the ground was too muddy. Finally, a barely acceptable weather window opened, and I powered up the tractor and set to work. After spending some time out front, I headed around the north end of the prairie. Making the turn back toward the house on the eastern trail, I noticed a conspicuous slippage. Steering became increasingly difficult until finally, on a slightly sloping portion of the trail, I ceased to find any traction at all and slipped closer to the tree line. Frustrated, I looked behind me and discovered the problem. One of the tires had disappeared. All I could see was metal rim, cutting a trench in the saturated ground. Somehow, it appeared that the tire had not only managed to go flat, it had slipped off. Closer inspection revealed that it had slid off to the inside and was loosely circumscribing the inner lip. Fetching a jack, I discovered that there was no leverage point against which to use it. That, and the back wheels kept rolling every time I tried. Cinder blocks, then, to chock the rearward progress, and then 2 X 12s to raise and platform the jack, but without success, I eventually ran out of ideas.

Hoping that another set of eyes could see a different solution I went next door and knocked, but my neighbor had the good sense to be away from home. Daylight was dwindling, albeit not as rapidly as my patience; dinner guests were on their way, and there I stood in brokenness and mud and wondered where I might find some dynamite at that time of day. Eventually, I detached the mowing deck, which revealed a purchase point for the jack, and the wheel/tire was eventually in my hand. But the ground was still muddy with the prospect of nighttime rain, the tractor was still precariously jacked, and I had no idea how any of it was going to go back together – that, assuming it all survived the night.

There was, as it turns out, a happy ending. The tractor remained high on the jack, the tire shop fixed the flat, I wrestled it all back onto the hub and lug-nutted it securely back in place. Despite the muddy ground, the slope, and my general incompetence, I maneuvered the mowing deck back onto the frame. All that, and much to my relief, I completed the balance of the yard. Steering the tractor back inside the barn, I turned off the ignition key, stepped down and heaved a sigh of relief. The tractor and I both out of harm's way. At least until next time.

But in the meantime, I acknowledged that I was making progress. Though God, according to Genesis, could simply speak a work and things were so, I am increasingly reconciled to the fact that despite my verbal preference, I have to use my hands.

This place just might make a farm hand out of me yet.


"WELL, YOU ARE A REAL FARMER," my friend David responded when I let him know I wouldn't need his help after all. Despite the fact that legitimate farmers everywhere are cringing from the association, I appreciated the affirmation. I was rather proud of myself as well.

Winter had succeeded autumn, and it had been snowing – almost a foot and a half of the stuff had settled upon us. It had been a week of the heaviest snow fall of the year, and quite possibly the heaviest in several years, and my tractor decided to sleep in. This would be the lawn tractor to which in winter is attached the 48" snow blower acquired for just such a week as this. Usually it roars into life and snaps right to work, doing anything I ask it to do. Within reason. But that morning, having suited up in full snow prophylactic gear and waded through the drifted tundra to the barn, I raised the overhead door, backed the tractor out with a roar and got half way through the job when it began to sputter and shutter and cough and belch out black smoke. Power plummeted, and after repeated attempts to power through the problem, I finally limped the equipment back inside.

I scratched my head. I consulted friends. We speculated that the diesel had turned to gel in the cold. I tried again the next day but was met with more of the same. Coughing myself, now, from the diesel exhaust, I called the service department at the equipment store and explained my plight. "You and everybody else," the man chuckled. "When did you buy your fuel," he asked.

I don't keep track of such things.

"Well, you might still be using summer blend."

Entirely possible. Who knew I was supposed to be emptying my tanks with the seasons?

He said a lot of other things about gel, additives, waxy build-up, ice crystals, etc., but most of it went over my head. I know a few things about the New Testament but very little about Kubotas beyond turning the key. He advised that I replace the fuel filters – both of them. Yes, it turns out that there are two. "The good news is that they are cheap."

I wasn't sure that was adequate consolation, "How much is the technician who comes home with me to put them in?"

More chuckling.

I wasn't kidding.

"Seriously, you expect someone like me, with a total dearth of mechanical prowess, to accomplish this task?"

He asked for a translation.

"You think an idiot like me can do this?"

"Well, probably," he responded without a whole lot of confidence.

That's when I contacted David to see if he could help. David knows about such things. He used to own a farm. Apparently, he still owns a tractor. Charitably, he agreed.

Yesterday, then, I circled by the dealership, picked up my two cheap filters along with every kind of fuel treatment in the shop, returned home, took a deep breath and mustered up resolve to make an attempt. Less than an hour later I emerged from the barn smelling like a refinery, a little contorted from having to stand on my head and pretzel my arms into spaces not designed for human access, but smiling and triumphant. I had actually done it.

By myself.

Without breaking anything.

Without profanity.

OK, without much profanity.

Somehow, while simultaneously thumping my chest and patting myself on the back, I managed to pour some of the fuel treatment into the tank for good measure before returning to the house to trumpet my success to my long-suffering and ever-encouraging wife. And to fire off an email letting David off the mechanical hook.

That's when he maligned the fraternity of farmers by including me among their numbers. Never mind. I'll accept the compliment even if it's only momentarily deserved.

That night I stopped at a station and refilled the can with fresh diesel – winter blend this time. We'll see what happens. It was only 8 below zero the next morning. What could possibly go wrong?

CHAPTER FOURTEEN

# SEASONAL TIME

*For everything there is a season, and a time for every matter under heaven: …a time to plant, and a time to pluck up what is planted.*

Ecclesiastes 3:1 (NRSV)

Yes, it's cold – 22 degrees according to the thermometer in the window. Balmy compared with some of the mornings we had already experienced in recent days, and nothing compared with the depths of winter that would surely come. Chilly, though, nonetheless. And yes, I had forgotten to wear my gloves – a careless mistake that would become more and more costly as the season progresses. But despite the discomforts I have come to rather like feeding the chickens on mornings such as this. They need me, after all. The feeders were empty and so I scooped the mash into the bucket and distributed it into the various tubes and boxes from which the girls – and SamtheRooster – spend these chilly days nibbling. They are increasingly dependent on my handouts as the austerity of winter descends. Their free-ranging, these days, affords little enough nourishment; the worms and bugs long-since having descended or departed to warmer climes. And so, I am attentive.

There are other ministrations. In recent days I had unloaded the annual supply of straw bales and stacked them around the chicken runs, creating a compostable barrier against the wind and eventual snow. That, and they love climbing the towers and enjoying the elevated view. Just in time I stretched the extension cords from the sockets at the solar panels to the warming waterers inside the coops. The "winterizing," in short, was largely done.

It is the daily work that remains and is ongoing. Repetitively resupplying the food and water. Stirring, refreshing, and occasionally replacing the bedding. Reconnoitering and repairing the fencing. Retrieving, perchance, a gifted egg. It is a rhythm. A life-sustaining discipline, along with releasing in the mornings and securing the hatches every evening. Clock work. Because if they are to survive, what I do matters. The fact of it – the concreteness of it – unlike in most other pursuits, is readily, viscerally, apparent – quite literally before my eyes and at my fingertips.

There is no appreciative feedback. They cluck no "thank yous" or nuzzle against my leg. SamtheRooster rather stalks around me, making clear his opinion that I am a nuisance intruder. Well and good. They have their work to do; I have mine. They have eggs to lay. I have coop bedding to refresh. They have food to eat and water to consume. I have those dispensers to keep full. Their job is to go about their living. Mine is keeping them alive. And the thanks I receive is not their mindful gratitude, but my own for the privilege of having a part to play in this great circle of things that purposes my getting up in the morning and paying attention throughout the day to basics like food, water, shelter and warmth and the lives that depend on them. From me, whether those lives are conscious of it or not.

And so, I get out of bed because I am conscious of it, and with numbing hands scoop the mash into the bucket and distribute it among the boxes and tubes all over again, suddenly and gratefully conscious, as well, of the other lives of which I have a part in keeping alive within this great circle of things. Cold hands and all.


THE MORNING CHORES ARE COMPLETE – later than usual, but not by my procrastination. Daylight didn't invite the work until almost 8 a.m., a dramatic shift from the 5 a.m. wake-up call only weeks ago. Even allowing for the seasonal shift, it's been interesting to note the more granular variations. Within the last week chicken bedtime has varied from 4:30 p.m. to 5:15 – incrementally later as we approach the winter solstice, rather than the earlier I would expect. Similarly, the morning release. Recent days have varied between 7 a.m. and this morning's bugle blow almost an hour later.

The girls don't seem to mind, neither SamtheRooster. Perhaps between the bitter cold nights and the persistent, possum problem, they are simply delighted to be alive and moving around at all. That delights me as well. Every morning I hold my breath when I release the latch and look inside to assess what price the flock might have paid for winter. Every evening I hesitantly, cautiously peek inside, bracing at the prospect of coming face to face with gray fur and egg-coated bared teeth rather than coos and feathers. So far, so good. The birds are cold-hardy breeds and shouldn't have a problem, but still. It's cold. I wouldn't want to trade places with them. As for the opossums, they are generally more interested in eggs, I have learned, than meat, but hunger has a funny and predictable way of tamping down our preferences. And I notice the distance the chickens maintain anytime one is around. Smart girls.

And so it is that I keep the feeders filled and the waterers topped off and plugged in to keep from freezing, and we collectively relish the absence of snow that keeps the flock sequestered and me frostbitten. As it is they are free to roam the range – inside the fence and, for the adventuresome, beyond. As long as they willingly return in the evening I don't really mind. They never go far, and their exploratory forays somehow make me smile. After all, I enjoy a new patch of ground every now and then, so I don't begrudge them their wanderlust. One of these days I'll get around to repairing the breach in the fence, but I'm really in no hurry. And who knows? Maybe all that extra exercise will shake loose a few more eggs now and then.

Snow will inevitably come, and the daylight hours will continue to shift one way and then the other. Each of those eventualities brings blessing and hardship. We will manage them as they come. Life in the country, after all, is more response than control – a kind of holy submission to forces infinitely larger and beyond us. Try as I might, I've so far not managed to move the sun. Or move the mercury beyond my walls.

Somehow I suspect the world is thusly better off.


YESTERDAY THERE WERE TWO; THE DAY BEFORE ONLY ONE. It's going that way. It doesn't take long or a very deep basket these days to gather eggs. Intellectually – and historically – I know that chickens require ample hours of light to produce eggs, and light is increasingly offered in diminishing doses as autumn leans toward winter. Nonetheless, the annual scarcity of these egg runs always leaves me feeling deprived; impoverished, even though I know that the myth of perpetual fecundity is a lie. Resourcefulness has its seasons.

It's not only the stingier light. The molt has set in among the coops – the chickens are losing their feathers; their usual colorful comeliness scragglified by bare patches, exposed quills and a pathetically bedraggled appearance. It's a natural, normal process of renewal and replenishment, but not an attractive one. And whatever energies and resources the hens might have retained for egg production is redirected to re-feathering. That's of pressing importance as temperatures fall and frost settles. Their semi-nakedness currently provides little insulation. I'll never understand why nature doesn't cycle molt through the summer when the girls would likely delight in a little nakedness, rather than the chilling close of the season more prone to shivering than sweating. But maybe there is a symmetry between falling leaves and losing feathers. It's all about renewal.

Before long they will all be fittingly replumed and ready to settle in for winter's differently paced assignments. Which is to say that fallow time is settling in on more than the garden and gardeners. Just as is the case with a high tunnel in the garden, it's possible to thwart the barrenness of the nesting boxes by adding artificial light to the coops. That's what the commercial houses do, and I'm content with the findings that the sustained production does the chickens no harm. It simply uses them up faster. Burns them out, so to speak, in a matter of seasons, and I have little interest in or incentive for that.

After all, if the image of the Taproot is to be more than a name on our sign – if it is to inspire us to reach deeper; if it is to signify our intentions to draw nourishment not available on the surface of life; if it is to encourage practices that build resilience – then encouraging us all, humans and hens and humus alike, to exhale more fully, to reach more deeply, to tend more sustainably, to drink from more remote and mineralized reservoirs rather than the surface waters, which run and evaporate, becomes not only a virtue, but also a lifestyle. Training ourselves to gather in the subterranean nourishment only available to those who give their roots the time and space to grow longer and downward is simply the blessed course of things here. More than a discipline we practice, the pattern of life here is a natural but essential rhythm practically forgotten in our culture's frenetic addiction to productivity that we are determined to counter-culturally model.

And so, we will not be selling eggs for the next few months. The hens – along with the rest of us – have deeper, more internal work to tend to. We'll all be better for it.

LAZINESS, PERHAPS, OR WIDER DISTRACTION. I could, of course, have just been lulled into complacency by the protracted mildness of the weather. There had been cold snaps, to be sure, and yet this punctuational final day of November found me once again coat-free – with a string of duplicate days yet predicted. Whatever the explanation, I still had not completed the winterization of the farm. The tools were largely organized and stored. The garden was officially put to bed, though the deer were claiming their biblical entitlement to any residual gleanings. More than a few had arced the fence – some clearing the clothesline strung above the fence while others showed off their precision with an airborne limbo through the foot-wide space between the fence and line. Finding one of the metal posts bent almost horizontal, I winced vicariously at the thought of some poor deer's scarred undercarriage.

It was the rain barrels that were delaying me. Two in the back near the garden; two in the front near the greenhouse. All four had acquitted themselves well; fall rains had filled them to capacity, and we would have need of their reserves, but not where they stood. The water in the barrels needed to be drained and relocated, while the barrels themselves must be brought into the barn for protection from freezing. They are plastic, after all – heavy and durable, but vulnerable nonetheless. Greenhouse seedlings would need a great deal of the water through the winter, and we had been filling as many gallon jugs as would fit, along with three plastic garbage barrels now swollen and lidded. Perhaps 130 gallons of rainwater had been safely gathered in. I hoped to store more. Though the front two barrels were greatly diminished, they weren't yet empty;

and the back two barrels were still holding their own. One thing was certain: it doesn't pay to try and move them with even a little water remaining.

Of course, I could just open the faucet and let the water drain out, and ultimately some of that would be necessary. But I was nagged by the stewardship of it. It felt like waste to simply have it trickle into oblivion. There is, I am aware, something irrational in that view. "Trickling away" is precisely what the rain intended those drops to do. I couldn't shake the sense, however, that it's somehow akin to letting lettuce rot in the crisper. It seems brazenly profligate – especially given the volumes of rural water we purchased through the drought of summer and desperately hosed onto the thirsty plants.

Perhaps in light of that drought-stricken memory – and having filled every container and available space – draining the barrels into the cracks of the rain's intended destination is stewardship of a different kind… Only briefly – and with the best of intentions – delayed.

A few weeks later, at a holiday gathering, a friend who lives with his family on a farmstead of their own, asked what my winter project would be this year. My conspicuously blank face apparently being adequate response, he went on to share that he identifies at least one big project he intends to complete each winter – partly to keep busy, but partly because the other more routine demands of the property are hibernating this time of year. Maybe equipment repair. Maybe organization of the tool shed. Maybe brush removal. Maybe, well, anything that gets neglected during the more hectic growing season.

I like the idea, and it presents better than, "I just want to relax," which is what I wanted to say. To be sure, I will need to peruse the seed catalogues, and tend to the care and feeding of the chickens.

Indeed, I've already winterized the coops with tarps and straw bales to keep snow and wind to a minimum in the runs, and I've switched out the waterers for the electric heated models. The girls (and one boy) have already appreciated the tarps and bales with Saturday's couple inches of snow. And with the nights in the single digits, the heated waterers are essential.

But those altogether routine assignments don't really have the ring of a true "winter project." Winter is also the season for farming conferences, and while we have plans to attend a few those don't adequately fit the category either. Garden planning must be accomplished as well – keeping track of seed purchases, eventually starting seeds in the greenhouse while snow is still on the ground, laying out the garden map online. And, if other parts of the year are focused on food production – growing, harvesting and preserving for later – this is that season for food consumption. Given what all we have laid aside in jars and in the freezer, that will be a major undertaking; hard work, eating all that beautiful harvest, but we were determined to face the challenge.

Over the ensuing days, however, I continued to think about the question, admitting that no one big, hairy, audacious project arose to command my attention or imagination. There are, however, smaller things – more interior work that easily gets neglected in the press of other things. My stack of books to read quickly reaches epic heights, and I could hope to whittle that down through the colder months. We had purchased two online classes that would focus us episodically through the season – one, a training course in fruit tree management that would certainly involve some practical application in winter pruning. And there are always writing projects – layered with the dust of sad neglect – those would be nice to brush off and move back to the center of my attentions and productions.

But I couldn't lie: that bit about "relaxing" wasn't just an off-handed, throw-away remark. I looked forward to taking fuller advantage of the longer nights and the shorter days. And if I happened to fall asleep with a book in my lap, it would give me something close at hand to do first thing in the morning.

WINTER, THE FALLOW SEASON, and it felt like I should be reading. Or something. These, after all, were quieter days. The mercury hovered around the single-digits, snow covered the ground and even the chores set aside for "slower times" were forgiven until it warmed. Except for the greenhouse plantings, this was the garden's fallow season when the earth's instinctual calisthenics quietly rejuvenate toward spring.

I should be doing the same – learning about seed selection, soil amendments, bug prevention, watering requirements, and why the cabbage leafed last summer but never formed a head; why not a single Brussels sprout seed germinated despite two separate plantings. Or, I could simply ponder the grace-filled wonder of the carrots – seeds that were a free gift accompanying the varietals I had actually ordered – planted and then largely forgotten, that became the surprise bounty of the fall rediscovered only as I was bedding the rows down for the winter. Or the tenacious generosity of the okra plants that never reached their bushy stature but nonetheless insisted on offering up their spiky fruitfulness from their gnomic twigs. Or the kindness of the deer who thoroughly inspected the garden confines up until the time I planted, and then disappeared, returning only after the harvest was completed.

Instead I flitted around the house like a hummingbird with ADHD, reading headlines but seldom the stories beneath them; returning books to the library only partially read; jumping into this while jumping out of that; eschewing complex sentences for mere subjects and predicates; sustaining an extended thought only under duress.

Perhaps it was the holiday season. Perhaps my abbreviated attention span was tracking with the shortness of the days. All I know is if I had been Morse Code I couldn't spell anything of consequence – all "shorts" and no "longs"; dots without dashes.

In pasta and bread making, we've been taught, there is the measuring and the mixing, the rising, perhaps, and even the resting; but eventually there is the kneading – folding the dough onto itself and then pressing into it with the heal of the hands; stretching, rolling, folding again and then pressing. Over and over again – the tactile paradox of gentleness and forcefulness – until the dough becomes itself, elastic but integral; firm but responsive. Kneading forms the gluten strands that give the dough structure and strength; they hold the pasta or the bread together. The proteins that are the gluten, of course, are already there; the kneading simply draws them together and develops them into long, resilient strands that lend the dough the character desired – that make fine pasta or bread truly "fine."

Perhaps, then, it's kneading I was needing – some imposed and methodical stretching to lengthen my constitutional strands. My body must be involved – sustained and challenging, sweat-producing movement – but similarly my spirit, where gluten of a very different sort needs stretching and working if I am to hold the whole of myself together. I didn't quite know how to go about it, but I knew there was a rhythm to it, a determined physicality, a rather disconcerting but satisfying stickiness, and a willingness to clean up the mess.

Those, and the enticing capacity to anticipate the results. It seems like good winter work.

For the body we joined a gym, signed up with a trainer and submitted to her paces. Twice each week she ran us, stretched us, and exhausted us. We gained strength and balance, and lost weight. The spirit, however, requires different calisthenics. Reading has always been my heavy-lifting of choice, but the books most recently stacked around me had been practical – the "how-to's" of leaning into this new life. This time called for pages of a different sort. I needed a different internal push and pull. Rationale. Philosophy. Comprehension, not just expertise. I read more Wendell Berry, the Kentucky farmer poet and essayist and novelist. I reached back to Aldo Leopold; further back to Henry David Thoreau; still further back to the teachings of scripture, which turns out to be full of eco-theology in ways I had overlooked before.

It was good winter work, indeed. Kneaded and strengthened, I looked forward to spring.

THERE IS AN IN-BETWEEN TIME THAT DOES NOT APPEAR on calendars or seasonal guides. Ambiguous, it is something past winter, but not quite spring. We lurch forward toward the garden, but are yet constrained by freezing nights and the occasional random snow. I feel myself teetering between the greenhouse and the garden. Anxious to begin in earnest with all the fruit and physicality the soil represents, I recede into the relative security of the sunny enclosure with its neatly lighted rows of sprouting seed cells and the concise sprinkles of the watering can. Not much can happen as long as the growth is confined there – but that's just it. Once transplanted to the garden, all kinds of things can happen; only a few of which are good. There are, in other words, opportunity costs to possibility.

Since late February I had been tending seeds – sorting the packages by germination requirements, sowing on schedule according to need, watering, warming, wooing and coaxing. Fiercely loving parenting, this pre-gardening business. The last of the seeds were finally nestled into their soil blocks, and the first of the tomatoes moved up to bigger digs.

Wispy cumin.

Recalcitrant eggplant.

Shy peppers

Exuberant chard.

Puppy-eyed Romanesco.

Reticent lavender.

Some have crept – patiently stretching yoga-like into vertical stem. Others erupted after little more than a kiss of the compost – animated by a raw and native joie de vivre. Some teased – keeping to themselves in subterranean mischief – until I had abandoned their prospects, condescending only then to emerge. Still others are, I am reconciled, stillborn. By now, however, every time the pups and I open the door and step inside that warm and moist horticultural cocoon the garden's foreshadowing is plain. And soon the reality of it – the perspirational, aspirational, and terrifyingly vulnerable work of it – will begin.

Which is what I ache for.

And dread.

All at the same time.

Wedged between winter and spring, then, this liminal space between safety and soaring.

Like so much of life.


The April air was still chilly outside, well on its way toward scraping the freezing mark predicted for later that night. It was likely to be among the last of such mercurial dips before spring managed a firmer hold of the season, but even so was arriving well past its welcome. Already real damage might have been done.

Blossoms already graced the fruit trees out back and the forsythia spangled the side yard and meadow, and the miscellaneous buds swelled on branches around the farmstead. A commercial operation might entertain certain interventions against the cold, but ours would have to suffer through on their own, surviving. Or not. This isn't business; this is nature.

Meanwhile, over the next few weeks the garden would demand increasing attention before planting and transplanting could begin in earnest – turning and tilling, cleaning and clearing and nourishing the soil to insure the most hospitable host for seedlings and seed. Already some 2,000 soil blocks were cradling germinating seeds in the greenhouse, with more to come – those in addition to the numerous varieties that would be directly seeded in the ground as soon as it was "safe."

As if, in growth and nature, any such concept like "safe" exists.

What we can do, however, is provide the best possible conditions within our control.

And so it was that, never mind the chill in the air, recent warm spells and the early morning showers offered adequate incentive to wield the broad fork in those garden rows still encumbered with last season's detritus – primarily gnarly stalks from cabbage and kale, cauliflower and broccoli. The funny thing was that despite the goose-pimply weather it felt good to be out there digging a bit. And pulling. Just as anticipated, the soil was damp and workable, and the roots and stalks slid out with only occasional protest.

But especially satisfying was the sense of the soil itself. When we first started digging this soil those several years ago it was dense, formidable, and full of clay. Over the ensuing years it had welcomed compost, manure, mulch and regular doses of home-stirred Complete Organic Fertilizer. It had been gently opened and respectfully planted. And, while it certainly still had room for improvement, more than once in recent days we had commented on the change. Instead of unfired pottery, it now looked like – soil. Even damp it had the capacity to crumble from one's hand instead of clumping into a stone.

But on this particular day, broad-forking the rows, I noticed more than felt. Worms. Thousands of worms. Every time we extracted a root the remaining hole was a-squiggle in retreating worms, offended by the sudden exposure.

Suddenly, despite the runny nose, it wasn't that chilly after all. Somehow it felt warm all over – and full of anticipation.

THOUGH THERE HADN'T BEEN MEASURABLE PRECIPITATION now in several days, my work boots kicked up sprays of dew trudging early out to the garden. Days had been warming, but the nights remained cool and heavy. That, and the ground was saturated. It had been difficult to get much cultivating done this year in preparation for the seedlings and seeds. Perhaps it was the last gasp of winter, the prior week's bonus snow fall, but wagering too heavily on that "last" part would never come with good odds. It wasn't even Mother's Day; who knew what yet could meteorologically happen? As some measure of my optimism, however, I had returned the snow shovel to its hook in the garage.

Anxious to seize this interruption of good weather, I grabbed the broad-fork and opened the fence. I had managed to till several of the rows the week before the weather reverted, but there was still much to do. I concentrated yesterday's available time on mixing up and distributing the organic fertilizer. On this day more muscles would be required. After bumping into descriptions and recommendations in my increasingly diverse readings, I had finally taken the plunge and ordered my own broad-fork – a very old, perhaps even ancient, completely manual farming implement designed to deeply loosen the soil. With its two sturdy handles and claw-like tines, the tool reaches down 14-inches, well below the churning capacity of a power tiller without turning the soil's basic architecture into a homogenized soup like the tiller.

But did I mention that it is completely manual? As in its only power comes from the upper body of the user. So, in other words, it's work. Basic, old-fashioned, physical work – the kind that makes you sleep well at night, at least after the ibuprofen has kicked in.

But I rather enjoy the effort. I can see what I have accomplished, I can comprehend and appreciate the intended value, and it feels at least symbolically like, with all this loosening, I am doing something redemptive. After all, the whole world is uptight, not just my garden. Neighbors and families, faith communities, and governing bodies – indeed whole nations – have become so hyper-sphinctered it's no wonder we pinball through our days intellectually and emotionally, morally and politically, militarily and interpersonally, flipping and colliding without ever really connecting. We are packed and wound tight.

A couple of hours later, I stuck the fork into the ground at the edge of the garden and leaned wearily on it, fully conscious of the exhaustion in my body, the accomplishment in the garden, and the serenity in my soul that my work was well done.

Later, prying off my dew-wet boots to go inside, I couldn't help wondering what the broad-fork equivalent might be for Congress and the rest of us in this hard-packed world who could similarly use a little loosening up, and an experience of soulful serenity at work well done.

I NO LONGER RECALL WHY I ORDERED THEM. I was reading something, no doubt, that extolled the virtues of Nanking Cherries and something apparently clicked. I do, after all, love cherries. Never mind that we had planted several cherry trees last year that should eventually supply more than enough fruit to meet our needs, these were different – a bush, for one thing, moreso than a tree. Requiring less space than trees and therefore more versatilely sited, they are reputed to be easy growers, not especially finicky about their surroundings, producing fruit – albeit smaller and therefore more difficult to harvest – comparatively fast. Gathering to myself all these compelling attributes, I seemingly tracked some down through an online nursery and placed an order.

I'm not proud of this horticultural impulsivity. I'm aware that one really should be more strategic and thoughtful about such considerations, as in thinking through where such new arrivals might actually be planted, and if, despite their attractiveness, they actually "fit in." But, that said, neither am I terribly penitent about it. We have space, we are curious and experimental, we value perennials and their fruit – for ourselves and the wildlife and pollinators – and we would find for them a place.

Unfortunately, they arrived during the recurring aftershocks of winter. They would need to camp out in the greenhouse.

Cutting the tape on the shipping container, I gently lifted away the moistened packing mulch and separated the bare root plants from each other. It was then I realized that not only had I been impulsive, I hadn't paid close attention to what I was doing. I had ordered three – already more than we needed – but it turns out that the "three" I had ordered were bundles of three. I'm not very good at math but even I know that adds up to nine. Nine bushes. We are really going to need to love Nanking Cherries. I settled the saplings into potting soil and tucked them into the greenhouse.

Winter had been a wearisome challenge. I happen to like winter. I will not willingly be one of those who packs the car, forwards the mail and heads off to warmer climates in an effort to bypass Iowa's harsher months. I like the snow, the fire in the fireplace, sweaters and flannel-lined jeans. I like snowshoeing the trails around and through the farmstead. I enjoy firing up the tractor and clearing the driveway after a heavy snowfall. But it can begin to wear, and we were feeling worn. There is a time and a place for winter which had expired a few weeks prior. Enough was enough. We had other things to do. It was, by this time, the middle of April and it had not only snowed in recent days, more was predicted for the coming days – never mind the 70-degree days in between. All this back-and-forthing made it impossible to move things into the garden, and even those sprouts in the greenhouse are yet timid about sticking their necks out very far.

Taking advantage of the day's sunny respite, I accomplished some plowing and garden bed preparation while Lori spread mulch and whacked away at some dying shrubs we will be replacing. We may or may not be able to squeeze more such preparations in tomorrow, depending on when the weather starts to deteriorate. Weary, with afternoon hours waning, we opted to water before going inside.

For the past month we had been sowing seeds in flats and settling them in the greenhouse. Thirty-six trays had so far accumulated there with likely that many more to go — trays of peppers and tomatoes, herbs and greens, flowers and leeks and now Nanking Cherries. Almost by rote now we fill milk jugs with rainwater stored through the winter, and tray by tray give everything a good dousing.

It was then that Lori noticed the cherries. The nine stems a few days ago had swelled proud buds, but on this evening there was one thing more: a blossom. The glory of Washington, D.C. in miniature. One lone blossom among nine budding stems. On the one hand there is nothing special about that. Fruit trees bloom, as apparently do fruit bushes. But parked there in a drink cup stuffed with potting mix and stowed in the greenhouse it seemed, nevertheless, almost bankable: a promissory note of spring, born of an impatience equal to my own; as if to say, "winter be damned, we are moving ahead with life."

And so it was that I decided to move forward with it, living rather than waiting; blooming, which is to say making way for fruit. Because for too many things to count –

in the garden,

  in my aspirations,

    in this crazy, "stuck" world,

      it is simply – if not past – time.

So, yes, we would find a place to plant the cherries. All of them.

As soon as the next round of snow melts.


I'LL CONFESS AT THE OUTSET THAT I HAVEN'T BEEN an attentive steward. All the guides I read stress the importance of keeping asparagus beds "clean" – as in weeded and free of herbaceous encroachment. Soil amendments wouldn't hurt either, like compost or other nourishing organic matter. I'm sure it's good advice, but I have neglected to follow it.

"Neglect," of course, is the proper description because ever since planting the two varieties of asparagus the first spring of our residence on the farmstead, I have been well-intentioned but poor-performing. Other, ever-pressing garden tasks this time of year annually assert a higher priority. Always. I must manage sprouts in the greenhouse, then I need to reposition the rain barrels after winter storage. The beds in the garden must be prepped for the seeds we directly sow, and then the seedlings started indoors must be transplanted. The irrigation lines must be run, rains inevitably interrupt us and…

Like I said, "Always." The asparagus always gets neglected. Perennially through these gardening years, this gem of spring has essentially had to fend for itself.

So, it is this grace-filled marvel that, inexplicably, it somehow manages, out of the morass of the previous year's detritus and this year's early weeds; despite creeping competition from nearby berry brambles; and ignoring grass from the pathways alongside, to emerge – these purple and green stems, at once delicate and sturdy. So pessimistic am I – along with inveterate distraction – the protuberances practically have to wave and shout and jump up and down to attract my attention. We happily take notice. Almost daily, with knife in hand, we navigate our way to those remote reaches of the garden to admire and avail ourselves of what growth the overnight has afforded. Even still I find it amazing, this tenacious generosity of soil and crown and time, made all the more miraculous by my neglect.

We do not take this beneficence for granted. We roast it, sauté it, grill it, and consume it raw. We include it in pastas, in frittatas,

and as the frame around steaks. In a word, we enjoy it.

I suspect all blessings are like that – testaments to unmerited grace. They simply present themselves unbidden and undeserved. The tomatoes and peppers, I dare say, I expect to harvest – along with all those other roots and fruits I so carefully coddle and tend. Indeed, I get annoyed when their output is sub-par. Harvesting them is my due, after all, given all I have invested in their growth. But the asparagus? By all rights those crowns I buried as a neophyte farmer all those years ago should have laughed at my fecklessness before lifelessly withering into the soil.

And yet, nonetheless, they appear, year after delicious year. As if to say, "I forgive you. Eat well. I'll do the best I can."

If I have any measure of gratitude, I will do all I can to do the same.

SOMETHING INHERENTLY WINSOME HAPPENS when filling your dinner plate with food that you have grown. And suddenly we were able to. The lettuce had been looking for an appreciative audience for a couple of weeks by this point in the summer; the squashes and tomatoes were just beginning to offer themselves. We snipped spinach and kale and chard last night for the first time and plucked several peppers along with a single prickly cucumber. All that, and it was clearly just getting started. It's as though the garden had taken a cue from the marketing slogan used by my beloved Blue Bell Ice Cream made at that "little creamery in Brenham, TX" – "Eat all you want; we'll make more." The miscellaneous bushes and vines were industriously making more.

The time had come to dig the garlic. The potatoes and carrots were well underway, and the okra was beginning to come on – miniature spears, at this point, that in no time would be finger-long and aching for the skillet. And the tomatoes were taunting – heavy orbs sagging the branches, tenaciously green and aloof; indifferently, or perhaps defiantly waiting for their day.

But that day would eventually come, and it would be the fruit of a partnership. Nature will have done the lion's share, of course, but I will have done my part – seeding, warming, watering and

lighting; transplanting and transplanting and tying and and protecting. And watching. Of that I have done more than my share.
Watching and waiting and tasting in my sleep.

Once upon a time, I have read, the seeds grew wild and free –
independent and reckless. The fields were a salad bowl; the ditches
were a tray; fence rows trellised whatever the birds had planted. But
with our domestication of the varieties has come a certain depen-
dence. They need us if they are to productively grow. Which is only
appropriate since it's becoming more and more plain that we need
them to productively thrive.

Clumsily, then, I do my part – at least the parts I know to do
while hopefully stumbling onto the rest of the things I need to do.
I will feed them in the trust that they, in turn, will return the favor.
Thus far, I think, I am getting the better end of the deal. In the
meantime, I feel more and more excited to see, each day, what will
be ready for dinner that night.


I HAD BEGUN TO THINK OF WEEDING AS SOMETHING akin to breath-
ing – or blinking – reflexive movements that one simply does without thinking too much about it. Second thought, however, corrects
that overly generous comparison. Unlike those bodily examples,
you don't have to do it. You can get by without devoting the time
and the energy. It is, finally, your privilege to make the choice. There
are consequences, to be sure, but not immediate ones. Weeding is
more "maintenance," in some sense of the word, and preventative
if given the longer view – which is to say that weeding is much
more like exercise. Or flossing. You know the dentist's dictum about
flossing: "You don't have to floss all your teeth; just the ones you want
to keep." The value of exercise, while perhaps not so cleverly stated,
is something of the same. Exercise – at least regular physical activity –
is only necessary to the degree that health is desired.

And so, I weed to keep the garden healthy so I can be healthy – so that the desirable growth can have its way with as little opposition as possible. It does nothing to prevent deleterious invasion, although some fungi and molds may, in the process, be held at bay. Insects are certainly not deterred by my attentions. But surely the slow and inexorable siphons and suffocations – those almost passive environmental decays of crowding and choking and shading and resource diversion – are defeated by my ministrations.

At least temporarily.

Perhaps that recognition is the gift of it all. Just as I cannot take one deep breath and be done with that task for the rest of the day or the rest of the week; just as I cannot perform a few calisthenics and be perpetually healthy; just as I cannot blink once and thereafter keep my eyes open, I cannot finally get the garden weeded. As soon as I complete the project, it demands resumption from the beginning. There is a dailiness to the work that echoes the rest of the best of life – the routinized discipline of attentive care, akin to regularly telling my wife, "I love you": saying it "once upon a time" doesn't quite suffice. Saying it today – or not – is consequential both for her and for me.

How much of life, I've begun to ask myself, is like weeding – not so much in its purging but in its constant invitation to pay attention and step into the fray?

Tomorrow I will resume the fingered attentions. Tonight I will breathe, blink, clean up, and do more than speak a word of love. I'll prepare a soothing cup of tea and make a special dinner for Lori who is currently nursing her second severe outbreak of poison ivy while reconsidering the wisdom – and price – of this crazy lifestyle and vocational choice we've made.

I'VE ALWAYS BEEN FASCINATED BY SECOND ACTS – people who intentionally or serendipitously reinvented themselves for a subsequent chapter of their life. I think of people like Ina Garten who was working as a nuclear budget analyst in the White House when she bought a small food store in Westhampton Beach, New York, called "The Barefoot Contessa" – the moniker by which she has ever since been known through her television cooking shows and string of published cookbooks.

I think of JK Rowling who started out adulthood as a researcher, later taught English as a second language in Portugal, eventually becoming a single mom on welfare when she began to write stories of a young wizard orphan boy named Harry Potter.

There are politicians, like John Glenn, who first orbited the earth as an astronaut and later walked the halls of the Senate chambers. Like Elizabeth Warren who was an elementary school teacher before she went to law school, practiced law out of her home, and after a few more turns, was elected to the United States Senate. And like Ronald Reagan, who was a radio sports broadcaster before becoming a film actor and ultimately President of the United States.

There are business types, like Jeff Bezos, who had a computer science career on Wall Street before launching Amazon.

There are star athletes who reinvent themselves, like OJ Simpson.... OK, maybe he's not the best example.

And there are ordinary types like Clara Peller, who was a manicurist in Chicago when she was hired as a temporary manicurist for a television commercial. One thing led to another and, after starring in a Wendy's Hamburger commercial asking the famous question, "Where's the beef?" went on to enjoy a second career as a character actor.

Second acts. Explosive second careers. "Re-wirements," as a friend of mine once put it, instead of "retirements." Putting oneself first to one use and then another. Less, "and finally;" more, "and then." Perhaps something like a preacher becoming a farmer.

Perhaps something like the garlic rows in the garden. Planted in October in a 12-row section in one zone of the garden and an 8-row "spillover" in another zone of the garden, we harvested the mature bulbs in mid-July. I feel a deep satisfaction, after all those months, to finally dig and pull and bundle all those aromatically bulbous stalks onto the empty shelves of the greenhouse to cure for storage. But it leaves a big vacancy in the garden – a mere half-way through the season.

We could, of course, start to coast. We could simply retire those sections until next year. After all, we have plenty growing in the other reaches of the garden. We have more than enough to do with what remains – weeding and watering, watching for bugs or diseases, gathering into the kitchen a thing or two as they ripen. And we have other interests and projects to occupy our time and imaginations. But leaving those spaces fallow seems like missed opportunity. There is still time before late autumn frosts and fertility in the soil. There are storage crops we would later appreciate. I ponder the question of stewardship and how we responsibly use ourselves and our resources.

And I'm haunted by the sound of Clara Peller's voice, asking over the image of that vast and empty bun, "Where's the beef?" knowing that, ultimately, she's not talking about hamburgers at all.

And so, we planted seeds in those vacant rows – beets and carrots, turnips and parsnips, fall cauliflower – and already salivate with the anticipation of a subsequent harvest.

A second act.

And wonder about seeds and empty rows of other and different and more significant sorts.


THE POTATO CORNER OF THE GARDEN matured into a surprise and a wonder. Occupying the five northwestern most rows, they included a like number of varieties – "Yukon Gold," "Yukon Gem," "German Butterball," "Red Thumb," names that roll off my tongue now, plus some unlabeled variety that was left over from last year and allowed to sprout in the basement storeroom like a Medusa village on the counter-top. At least those are the plantings that I knew about. Those trenches, it turns out, had more to offer than spuds alone.

I had noticed aberrational stalks and leaves as the plants began to emerge. Different shapes; different growth patterns; different colors than the rest – in virtually every row. I didn't think much about it earlier in the season, chalking up the variations to the vagaries of "nature" where, after all, not everything always matches. Eventually, however, the more fundamental dimensions of the differences refused any further glossing explanations. Something besides potatoes were presenting themselves. "Some-things" actually. Popping up here and there were plants that looked conspicuously squash-like. And then there was something else – familiar looking, but (incredulously now, looking back) I couldn't name. I watched; and waited. And all of it grew – the potatoes, the unidentified squash-like vines, and the mystery foliage. There is, I now recognized, even a marigold variety popping up that I had grown from seed last year in the greenhouse.

When tomatillos began to emerge from the branches of the mystery bush, that "mystery" was solved. How I failed to make that identification earlier baffles me since there are multiples of them growing elsewhere in the garden. But that "elsewhere" qualifier was an equal part of my surprise. There were, indeed, some tomatillo bushes planted in those rows last summer, though they never amounted to much. In fact, I counted that prior season's tomatillo crop a failure. Apparently, the remnants rallied over the winter, in search of horticultural redemption.

The other interloping plant presented more of a puzzlement. They were, indeed, a squash-like plant, with bright yellow blossoms, just like the zucchinis and yellow straight-necks. Then, nestled low and largely hidden by the vines and the encroaching grasses, I discovered maturing several white pumpkin-like fruits. Thus far the size of a baseball, I hadn't a clue what to make of them. I planted no such varietal last year or this. There were some winter squash seeds I planted far too late last fall, but they were sown on the front side of the garden 50 feet away, and were ultimately ravaged by frost shortly after blossom set. I neither recognized this fruit, nor could fathom how it came to grow in this spot – in multiples. Rabbits, I suppose; or birds moving things around in one way or another – but from where? And when?

The questions, of course, are curiosity rather than concern. I count the misplaced plants a grace – like discovering an Easter egg in October. Seeds, after all, are meant to grow and these had miraculously managed to succeed at it. I could only be grateful that they found a habitable soil and hospitable neighbors, and we looked forward to enjoying the fruitful precipitate of their sojourn.

And in the future, I would put an asterisk in my garden planner beside the names of seeds I've purchased and sown. "These," my footnote will clarify, "are only what I know to be planted." It's anyone's guess what all might really emerge.

STANDING OVER A WEED-INFESTED ROW, nudging along the blade of a hoe, I pause to consider the progress – my own with the weeds, and also that of the vegetable starts I'm tending. I had naively and ambitiously agreed to furnish vegetables for a restaurant dinner later in the summer, but I was resisting the pressing need to provide a tentative inventory of what the chef might reasonably expect from our garden. I knew what we had planted, and I could observe what seemed to be thriving. But I am still a horticultural neophyte. I have yet to evolve that intuitive inner calendar that simply knows when things are due. Moreover, I had so far procrastinated on developing the good and helpful habit of maintaining annual garden notes, which means I didn't even have the benefit of our prior years' experience beyond simple anecdotal memory; and that didn't feel like much to bank on. Never strong enough to lean on, my recollections are only getting fuzzier. And while, yes, I can read the seed packets for their statistical predictions and norms, that, too, has its limitations.

Growth, after all, is a mysteriously mercurial thing. The copywriter who added those cultivation notes to the catalog and seed packet – presumably drawing on rich and deep expertise – nonetheless doesn't live on our property, doesn't dig in our soil, and may or may not water at the same rate as I do. And even if I had kept growing notes from previous seasons, I have learned the hard way that seasons rarely Xerox themselves for later use. Each one is its own work of art with its own brush strokes and hues. There are variables.

All that, plus the fact that plants are living things with their own strengths and idiosyncrasies. Standing over an adolescent vine prognosticating about its progeny feels about as predictive as speculating on the future career of an 8th grader. Or, for that matter, a 62-year-old. We change, after all. Or flame out. Or catch a different spark. Or. Who knows in advance exactly what will grow? Or when it might mature?

I liked the looks of the radicchio, but having never grown it before I have no clear guess about any harvest. The garlic and the wheat would soon be coming out, but the cabbages were a long way off. I could see blossoms on the squashes and green beans, but I couldn't venture a guess as to how many and by what date. The braising greens we could count on, but a meal requires more than kale and collards and chard; and there was little hope that the peppers and tomatoes would be there to play a supporting role. Cucumbers? Probably, but we would have to see. Even if I'm not quite sure what it would be, something good would show up in the kitchen in ample time to serve

Everything is a work in progress.


AND SO IT GOES. THE REPETITIVE RHYTHM OF THIS LIFE AND WORK. The seasons, the dreaming, the preparations, the repairs; the sowing, the weeding, the harvesting; the constant alternation between hope and despair, too much and not enough, gratitude and disappointment.

We pray. Ultimately, we dig deeply into ourselves for the patience and larger view this kind of endeavor teaches and daily demands. I think of that biblical admission from the Apostle Paul – in a rare moment of humility and in the midst of one of those early church rivalries – that, "I planted, Apollos watered, but God gives the growth." Which is to say that none of us is in charge of it all. We do what we can do, and then let go.

As the season comes around again, we will once again see what might grow – through our efforts and all those which are beyond us. We will see what might happen because of us, in spite of us, or coincidental to us.

We will do our part, acknowledging that the bigger part is out of our hands. Which is humbling, of course, but that is the truth about most things in our life. We sow a seed. Someone else waters. Something else – something marvelously, mysteriously, ineffably beyond us – gives it growth.

It is maddening, I suppose, to good bootstrap-pulling, self-reliant delusionals reared to believe we can do anything and all. But it is, quite simply, the actual way things work. If I quiet myself enough to hear her, I hear the earth gently and lovingly chastising and coaxing me with the simple invitation:

"Get over yourself, take a deep breath, and simply participate in the wonder of what is transpiring."

We shall see. Listening just now to the thundering rain that simultaneously nourishes, drowns, washes away and keeps us out of the garden, we can do little else.

# CHAPTER FIFTEEN

# CONCLUSION

*Do not depend on the hope of results...*
*[Y]ou may have to face the fact that your work will be apparently*
*worthless and even achieve no result at all, if not perhaps results*
*opposite to what you expect. As you get used to this idea, you start*
*more and more to concentrate not on the results, but on the value, the*
*rightness, the truth of the work itself.*

Thomas Merton

S o what?

　　We have been answering this still-somewhat baffling call
to the land for almost eight years now. We have become well-acquainted with a handful of preferred seed purveyors, and increasingly familiar with particular varietals of vegetables. We have become
attuned to the pitch pipe of the seasons, bending our schedules and
timing our tasks to harmonize with the seasons and their particular needs and opportunities. Garlic, we have learned, goes in the
ground in October and is harvested in July, a few weeks after we
have harvested the scapes from the hardnecks (all terms that were
meaningless to me just a few short years ago) once we see the foliage yellow and die back. Fruit trees are pruned in late winter, just

before we start the early seeds in the greenhouse. I've learned that we live in growing zone 5 and the relevance of average last and first freeze dates. I've also learned that this is changing.

Climate change means that our zone 5 will likely shift gradually into zone 6 and those average freeze dates will spread accordingly. That may not sound significant, but coupled with the increasing severity of storms and the widely, wildly fluctuating variations of rain and drought, the adaptations required will be more than incidental. At the local level, plant varietals we have become adept at growing will have to be replaced by more heat tolerant ones with which we have little experience. Entirely new bug pressures will be experienced as different, potentially more destructive species find in our warming environs a habitable home. Internationally, water wars are already being fought. Already devastating winds and floods are more and more commonplace. While I have been reluctant to impose my mark on this small plot of land, we as human cultures continue to be cavalier about the morality and impact of fundamentally altering our climate; apathetic about the implications those changes will wreak. We have important and collective work to do.

Meanwhile, I'm still internalizing maturity patterns of the myriad vegetables we plant – a task that would be made routine if I would simply take the time to note on my calendar the growing days commonly referenced on seed packets – but my internal calendar is gradually finding a general calibration.

We are, to put a point on it all, growing; and learning. That says something, but not ultimately enough. Our objective in moving to this expanse of soil with a shovel in hand was to learn how to grow food on simpler terms than those employed by the larger, now conventional food system that I deem to be unsustainable. And we are learning.

Along the way we have necessarily expanded our course of study to include soil microbial activity and organic matter content, pollinator attraction and habitat, naturally beneficial ecosystem development and enhancement, climate fluctuations, and more. We have grown familiar with the reproductive patterns of deer and rabbits; the predatory hours of raccoons and opossums; the sunlight requirements for laying hens and the value of the preserving "bloom" that naturally coats a freshly laid egg. We have observed how rainfall moves on our land, prevailing wind patterns, and the value of "edge zones." And we have experienced the joy – and the burdensome responsibility – of harvest. After all, having invested time, energy and months of attention we want nothing to go to waste. And our freezers are full – the plural-denoting "s" on that noun being intentional. We are physically stronger, healthier and, according to the comments of friends and verified by our updated driver's license photographs, younger. We have lots to smile about, and happily and routinely we do.

All that being said, we are no stranger to the grocery store. And it can be depressing. Passing through the produce department, mentally comparing the softball-size bell peppers, the foot-long carrots, the shoe-size potatoes, the spotless apples with my punier, more blemished counterparts, it's hard to feel like a success. Our results feel – paltry.

And then, I remind myself that there is more involved than our inexperience. We have consciously chosen to use older, typically heirloom seeds rather than the modern, proprietary hybridized varieties. We have eschewed herbicides, pesticides, and synthetic fertilizers that function like steroids in athletes – all choices that we fully realize mean harder work, smaller and fewer and less beautiful expressions.

Why, then?

Part of the answer is because we have come to believe it to be important. Something deep down has persuaded us, along with Merton, that some things are more important than results. I know that sounds heretical in 21st century America, where "bigger, faster, cheaper, more" is our real national anthem. But despite the drumbeating mantra of the marketing forces at play, we have learned the hard way that "new and improved" are not synonyms. While there are certainly and blessedly beneficial innovations, today's breakthrough solutions have a nasty way of turning into tomorrow's intractable problems. Lori and I have developed an aversion to the idea of eating food that has been bathed in toxic sprays; a bias for vegetables that have been selected for flavor rather than appearance and durability for long-distance shipping; and a principled preference for open-pollinated seeds over patent-protected hybrids, believing that something as fundamental as fruits and vegetables should be the common "intellectual property" of us all.

I SUSPECT I'LL ALWAYS FEEL SOME MEASURE OF "PEPPER ENVY" while passing through the produce aisles of the grocery store, admiring the size and the visual perfection. But I wouldn't trade our smaller, gnarlier harvest from our own garden. Fresher, healthier and tastier, it ultimately digests as something yet more: our own determination to concentrate, as Merton implored, less on the results, and "more and more, on the value, the rightness, the truth of the work itself."

And that tastes pretty darn good.

We have learned larger lessons as well.

- Chickens are smarter than most people think.

- The earth is full of life.

- The earth abounds in grace.

- There is no such thing as waste.

- The circle of the seasons emulates the circle of all life processes.

- Nature has experience with healing, adapting, and thriving – and will do so, though not necessarily in ways that will support human flourishing.

- Nature holds a vast supply of wisdom for those who are willing, observant, and humble enough to learn.

- We keep in mind the intrinsic connection between humus, human, humility, and humor to our common benefit.

- Human well-being thrives on a balanced interplay of mental, spiritual, and physical exercise – the latter preferably outdoors.

- Learning in the second half of life can be at least as exhilarating as in the first – and just as filled with awe.

CURIOUSLY, THIS NEW LEARNING HAS EXTENDED into my old calling. In the years since leaving full-time parish ministry I have occasionally been drawn back to fill in temporarily with various congregations; sometimes for a day, occasionally for a season, and in one case almost two years. I have been surprised not by how easily I slipped back into the role, but at how different is the lens through which I see the work. No longer concerned with the organizational burdens of funding and management; no longer preoccupied with the institutional details of programming and denominational fidelity; no longer expected to "cast a vision" or provide leadership at all beyond the prescribed needs that brought me into these brief relationships, I find myself processing these liturgical opportunities as agricultural ones. The dynamic is less teaching and learning, less leading and following, and more cultivating and growing.

Jesus once told a parable about a sower who went out to sow. The seed scattered everywhere – on a path, on rocky ground, among thorns, and into good soil. Looking out over the congregation at an earlier stage of my ministry, I mentally assigned those soil types to the faces looking back at me. After these few years actually working with soil and sowing seeds, the judgments no longer seem relevant. Soil, I've learned, is hardly static. The worst soil can be rehabilitated; the richest soil can be depleted.

I sow seeds in these circumstances – theological, spiritual ones in this case – and do what I can, not only to encourage their growth, but to improve the soil, comprehending now what I didn't understand before: that some of the smelliest parts of our interactions can ultimately and with patience become, like compost, the most beneficial.

We are, then, learning; but yet something more. I noted in the beginning that we had no intention of being changed, but of course it has happened. We have, under the inspiration of the growing seasons of vegetables and trees, become more patient and with a view toward more distant horizons. We think more organically and with a sharpened instinct for mutual benefit, not just in the garden but in every aspect of our lives. We live more generously and, as befits our earthy origins, more humbly; amazed by the grace and abundance that nature offers up – in eggs and vegetables and fruits, to be sure, but in resilience, generativity, beauty and diversity. Not only have our fields of endeavor changed, but in the sowing and reaping, the tilling and tending, the reading and experimenting and failing and trying again, our very taproots themselves have changed. We have, indeed, grown deeper, sturdier, at once larger and tinier as we continue to comprehend the beautiful immensity of this creation of which we are a part.

Yet one traceable point remains outstanding. I said that we moved here to learn how to grow food on simpler terms. That is only partially true. I felt called – not only to learn, but to pass along this foundational, sustaining wisdom to succeeding generations with at least a breath of encouragement and inspiration. We have succeeded in planting a few gardens and tending a few chickens. Whether or not we have succeeded at this more important goal remains to be seen. Those who have read this far will answer that question by what you do next.

I hope you will plant something – something to eat, like a squash, something to admire, like a flower, something to change your world, like an idea – partly for the sheer joy of watching it grow, and partly as a down payment on the wondrous gift of providing food for body and soul for yourself and others that is truly good. We took a giant leap, but that isn't necessary. You don't need to quit your job and move to the country. Visit a farm or linger a bit at the local farmers' market and talk to growers about what they do. And why, reading the satisfaction in their eyes only slightly dampened by fatigue.

An earthier step might be possible. If you have a lawn, you can partition off a portion for a garden. If you don't have a lawn, perhaps you have a flower bed that can be reimagined. If you don't have a flower bed, perhaps a single pot you can fill with soil and a seed. The seed packet will teach you how. If you have a fragile idea that cries out for you to let it grow, find its metaphoric seed package for guidance and take the risk. Do it. Whether or not it grows, whether or not your efforts come to fruition, you will learn to pay a different kind of attention to the power of hope, the exhilaration of anticipation, the rhythms and vulnerabilities of life itself. And you may, indeed, grow dinner.

# POSTSCRIPT

When I answered this call to life and ministry on different terms, I was, as chronicled in these pages, as green as the leaves and stems I hoped to encourage. I had no prior experience with such work; no insight; no real clarity about how to begin - only the shallowest book knowledge. We simply moved to the farmstead and started trying. And once again attending meetings, this time around with farmers both locally and around the country.

While it is true that I have never been around quite this much denim and plaid flannel, it is even more true that I have never been around more open-hearted, open-handed people. Never have I known a community more generous with their knowledge, more patient with questions, more encouraging to beginners, and more relationally open to newcomers. Information and experience are to be happily shared, not jealously guarded like trade secrets. They – we – help each other erect hoop houses, crowd-source problem solving suggestions, selflessly circulate plant trial results, compare notes on varietal choices, and share tool suggestions. This is a gracious community, without which I would still be wondering how deep in the ground I should poke a seed.

I wonder sometimes if disagreements about methods and technologies arise, if jealousies crop up, if competition at the local farmers' market digs into their camaraderie. I don't know. I just know that the sense of community and helpfulness among them has drawn me to them. I can only speculate where this preference for generosity comes from, but I suspect that they, too - having been the recipients of patient counsel and aid in their own novice years - feel a certain obligation to share information and find joy in passing it on.

To all those patient souls who have responded to my panicked text messages, who have helped identify bugs and recommended supply sources, who have volunteered to help and made room for me at the conference table and at the lunch table, and who encouraged me to break out my own denim and plaid, to you I am forever grateful. And still learning.

As FOR THE TWO OF US, something odd and quite apart from the learning has occurred. In response to this surprising, soul-filling call, we left home – the house we enjoyed, the work we had known, the norms and habits of a lifetime – and set off in a new direction. In the ensuing years and over the bumps and dips of learning and familiarity, we have inexplicably arrived home – home, of course, being an enigmatic concept. As I observed in the beginning of these pages, collectively we are not of one mind on the subject. Home is variously where we grew up, where we are or where we are hoping eventually to arrive. For some it is where the heart is.

For others it is that place to which you can never return or, for still others, that locus to which one must eventually return for life to be fulfilled. Conflictually defined as a location, a shelter or a community, we seem only able to agree that home is where we belong. With all due respect to Thomas Wolfe's famous dictum that, "You can't go home again," I am increasingly convinced that "home" is that place from which we cannot stand to be absent for very long.

In the course of these years at Taproot Garden, I have come to know home as that experience of groundedness – where I know myself in a deep and authentic way and from which I see the world around me more honestly. I speak of it as "there" only because I have not found a more suitable term of reference. It is, after all, less a particular geography locatable by GPS coordinates, but rather a more clarified state of being; a stabilizing, if inarticulate, sense of "yes" – an exhalation.

Settling down on this piece of ground we named Taproot Garden, we were palpably aware of our inexperience but also of an invitational fecundity that beckoned our own taproots. And so we planted – seeds, to be sure, and trees – but ourselves, as well, along with our aspirations and comprehensions. The prairie grasses and apple trees have grown and matured, and we along side them, it seems. We have grown as farmers, as stewards of this land, but also as people.

Spring is again unfolding and our attentions return to the garden. It is a frenzied season, finding intervals between the rains to refresh garden beds and transplant seedlings from the greenhouse. In the cool of the evening, however, we take a break to stroll again the prairie path, as we had on that first Christmas afternoon of our residence here.

In the ensuing years the rough and partial path has been shaped and completed. We think again of the Magi from the biblical story.

Like them, we left home with little more than a vague dream and the propelling wonder of *naïveté* and traveled some distance along a surprising and unexpected route. We, too, encountered problems and received guiding wisdom from unexpected sources. And, like the Magi, we, too, have found our way home by another way, where we have surprisingly, comfortably, and gratefully put down deep and securing roots.

ßß

# Acknowledgements

Special thanks to L.T. and Ahilia Bhramdat of L.T. Organic Farm in Waukee, Iowa, and Angela Tedesco of Turtle Farm in Granger, Iowa, who welcomed us to their farms and provided us our first introduction to the weekly wonders of a Community Supported Agriculture box. Through you we came to eat well and live better, and aspire to something more.

Profound thanks to Mary Y. Nilsen, encouraging friend and nudging editor, whose shaping thoughts, careful eye, and poetic sense not only weeded and pruned and watered these words into a book, but a tastier one than I ever dreamed of growing.

# BIBLIOGRAPHY

Beresford-Kroeger, Diana. *The Global Forest: 40 Ways Trees Can Save Us.* New York, NY: Penguin Books, 2010.

Berry, Wendell. *Imagination in Place.* Berkeley, CA: Counterpoint Books, 2010.

Berry, Wendell. *The Art of Loading Brush: New Agrarian Writings.* Berkeley, CA: Counterpoint, 2017.

Berry, Wendell. *New and Collected Poems.* Berkeley, CA: Counterpoint, 2012.

Blair, Katrina. *The Wild Wisdom of Weeds: 13 Essential Plants for Human Survival.* White River Junction, VT: Chelsea Green, 2014.

Commoner, Barry. *The Closing Circle: Nature, Man & Technology.* New York, NY: Alfred A. Knopf, 1971.

Grahm, Randall. *Been Doon So Long.* Berkeley, CA: University of California Press, 2009.

Howard, Albert. *An Agricultural Testament.* Benediction Classics, 2010.

Kessler, Brad. *Goat Song A Seasonal Life, A Short History of Herding, and the Art of Making Cheese.* New York, NY: Scribner, 2009.
Kingsolver, Barbara. Animal Vegetable, Miracle: A Year of Food Life. New York, NY: HarperCollins, 2007

Leopold, Aldo. *A Sand County Almanac: And Sketches Here and There.* New York, NY: Oxford University Press, 1949

Logsdon, Gene. *Holy Shit: Managing Manure to Save Mankind.* White River Junction, VT: Chelsea Green, 2010.

Lowdermilk, Inez Marks. *All in a Lifetime: An Autobiography.* Berkeley, CA: *The Lowdermilk Trust,* 1983.

David R. Montgomery. *Dirt: The Erosion of Civilizations.* Berkeley: University of California Press, 2007.

Montgomery, David R., and Anne Bikle. *The Hidden Half of Nature: The Microbial Roots of Life and Health.* New York, NY: W.W. Norton, 2016.

Robinson, Marilynne. *Home.* New York, NY: Farrar, Straus and Giroux, 2008.

Sanders, Scott Russell. *Staying Put: Making A Home in a Restless World.* Boston: Beacon Press, 1993.

Tall, Deborah. *From Where We Stand: Recovering a Sense of Place.* Baltimore, MD: Johns Hopkins University Press, 1993.

Thoreau, Henry David. *Walden; or, Life in the Woods.* Boston, MA: Ticknor and Fields, 1854.

Tickell, Josh and John Mackey. *Kiss the Ground: How the Food You Eat Can Reverse Climate Change, Heal Your Body & Ultimately Save Our World.* New York, NY: Simon & Schuster, 2017.

Trubek, Amy B. *The Taste of Place: A Cultural Journey Into Terroir.* Berkeley, CA: University of California Press, 2008.

Warner, Charles Dudley. *My Summer in a Garden.* New York, NY: Random House, 2002.

Wohlleben, Peter. *The Hidden Life of Trees: What They Feel, How They Communicate.* Vancouver, B.C.: Greystone Books, 2015.

Made in the USA
Middletown, DE
22 June 2019